PERSEVERANCE

The Bridge to a Latina Mother's Dream

Iris V. Fernández

ROSALES MAVERICKS
PUBLISHING STUDIO

Las Vegas | New York | Mexico

Title: PERSEVERANCE

Subtitle: The Bridge to a Latina Mother's Dream

IDENTIFIERS

ISBN: 978-1-959471-35-6 (English Paperback)

ISBN: 978-1-959471-44-8 (English Hardback)

ISBN: 978-1-959471-43-1 (English Digital)

Library of Congress Control Number: 2024902039

Categories: Memoir, Latina, Women

Cover design by: Taína Carrero

Editor: Hadassa Muñoz Rivera

Printed in the Las Vegas, Nevada, United States of America

ORDERING INFORMATION: Iris V. Fernández
www.irislablanca.com

PUBLISHER: RMPStudio™ www.Adriana.Company

DEDICATION

This book is dedicated to my Light, Taína Carrero. I am profoundly honored that my daughter chose me to be her mother. From the moment of her birth, she has been my source of unwavering strength and guidance.

During the storms of life, nursing her brought instant calm and an unbreakable bond. In her elementary school days, she bore the weight of bullying silently, never wanting to disrupt my studies. Through her young adulthood, her wise insights illuminated my personal life. Today, as an adult, she remains my light and rock. Her warrior spirit and authentic nature fill me with pride and admiration.

She is not just my cherished daughter, but also my trusted friend. Taína has journeyed through my somewhat turbulent life, emerging stronger and more resilient.

With all my love,

Mommy

"…the most beautiful sound I ever heard, Taína!!..

Contents

AUTHOR'S NOTE

This book is entirely based on how I remember my youth and dialogues back then. I have disguised names, characters, and situations to protect the innocent and not-so-innocent.

And yes, all are forgiven, even me!

FOREWORD

I first met Iris not long after she had retired and was immediately struck by her clarity of purpose; she wanted to write her memoir. Her reasoning was that she would share her story to offer hope and inspiration to other women.

Maintaining a focus to turn your dreams of penning your memoir into a reality is not easy, yet Iris has succeeded despite bumps in the road. She is a woman of substance, a woman who has stepped fully into her power, claimed her identity, and owned her own life, mistakes, and all.

Between the pages of *Perseverance: The Bridge to a Latina Mother's Dream,* we are taken on a journey that sees a naive, innocent young girl learning life's lessons the hard way. Domestic violence, poor choices in partners, and reliance on food stamps to feed her family are enough to have made anyone quit and give up on their dreams. Instead, Iris dug in her heels, demonstrating through her life's journey that when we persevere, we can surmount any challenge and emerge on the other side, tougher and more tenacious than before.

In this captivating memoir, Iris shares her life story, a testament to the importance of believing in oneself, listening to one's inner voice, and the power of perseverance to make dreams a reality by following a pathway.

Perseverance requires courage, determination, and love. These have been the foundation upon which she has built her life. The love for her children, the love of her family and her love of providing service to others, using her talents as a nurse and advocate.

It has been my privilege to watch Iris travel her journey over the past few years and witness her transform from tentatively putting her toes into the writing world by submitting short pieces into a confident writer, standing in her own space, listening to her heart, and following her dream to publish her memoir.

With admiration and respect.

Michelle Hanton OAM
Business Strategist
December 2023

ACKNOWLEDGEMENTS

Where do I begin? I hope I am not missing anyone.

First, I want to thank Source, my Creator, for always conspiring on my behalf. I am eternally grateful to Mami and Papi, Virginia, and Manuel Fernández for accepting being my parents and the 500 ancestors who all contributed to my DNA.

Thank you, my daughter, Taína Carrero, for all your support, as the best daughter and as my first 'editor' at the beginning of this project. I love your entrepreneurial spirit and your technological expertise that have anchored me through the writing of this book.

Venus, Ilene, and all the resilient mothers, biological and spiritual, young and old, navigating life through all their peaks and valleys. You have inspired me to complete this work! Although it may not seem like it now, you are already winning! Your loved ones are the beneficiaries of all your compassion and devotion.

I cannot leave out my mentor and greatest supporter through those Southern years, Mr. Jim Barber, who, until recently, was still working at Southern Ct State University. He encouraged me to persist in my quest to graduate with my BSN. He also planted that seed in me to write a memoir before I graduated in 1985.

I wish to thank Michelle Hanton of the Dragon Sisters who started this journey with me after taking the Hay

House 7-Day Writing Challenge and creating the FB Group as a supportive place dedicated to connecting, supporting, and providing accountability specifically focused on novice writers. Through this group, I have met other talented writers, and I remained accountable for continued writing and submitting stories to various competitions and publishing in four anthologies since 2020. I value Michelle's continued support throughout these years.

I would be remiss if I did not mention Denise Soler Cox and Project Enye and Irisneri Alicea, an amazing Genealogist, who has helped with my hobby of keeping up with my ancestral tree. Denise also introduced me to Adriana Rosales and the Latinas 100^{TM} community, launching me into my author career after retirement from nursing. Adriana has nurtured and encouraged me to write my stories in vols 2 and 3. I am grateful for this like-minded community, especially Hadassa Muñoz-Rivera, who is not only my editor but now a sister-friend. I have been able to write from my heart and share my joys and my sorrows with Hadassa, my kindred spirit.

Adriana introduced me to Claudia Romo Edelman of We Are All Human and Hispanic Stars Rising and I have now published stories in vols III and IV of Hispanic Stars Rising, The New Face of Power. I am indebted to Claudia for the opportunity to publish my work and help bring my voice to the Latinx community while I completed my memoir.

In memory of Corey Dean Arcelay, MD 1955 - 2019

INTRODUCTION

Thank you for selecting this book out of all the ones you could have chosen. I hope that by sharing my journey with you, you may learn ways to follow your aspirations, whatever they may be, no matter where you are in your quest.

I am not a well-known celebrity who underwent some life-altering transformation... I am just one ordinary "Nuyorican" from the projects in the South Bronx who managed to pursue a viable career as a graduate Registered Nurse despite some poor choices in life, like becoming an HS dropout and a teen single mom in the 1970s.

There were additional challenges in the age before the World Wide Web and Google. My working-class family did not have a house or a car, but we had each other.

Looking back on my life, I would not change anything since there was a lesson to be learned in every adversity. If you, my reader, can benefit from my life lessons without having to experience the adversities, then my journey was not for naught. That being said, let me define bridges as a metaphor:

Bridges represent connections, transitions, and the ability to overcome obstacles in life. They symbolize the passage from one phase to another, the crossing of boundaries, and the bridging of gaps between people, ideas, or situations. Bridges as metaphors often emphasize the importance of building relationships, finding common ground, and fostering understanding and cooperation. They signify resilience, adaptability, and the capacity to navigate challenges and transitions with grace and strength. Bridges in this context represent opportunities for growth, personal development, and the bridging of differences to create harmony and unity.

Let me share some of those connections and transitions in my quest to overcome some of life's obstacles…

PART I: At First

"Change is inevitable. Growth is optional."

John C. Maxwell

Chapter One

"Success is not final, failure is not fatal: It is the courage to continue that counts."

Winston Churchill

Teen Dropout Mom

Hello Reader, let me share a little about how I became a teen mom and dropout in 1972...

My "marriage" lasted 18 months! On Labor Day weekend of 1973, my husband left me penniless, without a diploma, and with a 1-year-old toddler to care for. I had quit high school in the middle of my junior year when I found out I was pregnant. It broke my heart to disappoint Mami. "Mi hija, porque?" Mami had wanted me to date other young men and finish my high school education so I wouldn't have to depend on anyone but myself, but I was in my fairy tale existence and felt that I didn't need to be on my own, after all I would now be married, and I would have my very own baby to care for soon. "What did I need an education for?"

Hindsight is 20-20! Do you ever look back at choices you've made and say, 'Yeah, I shouldn't have done that!' Mami's advice was for my good, anyway.

My husband was then a construction worker at the World Trade Center, and he would take care of us, or so I thought. They laid him off before my son was born. We were then eligible for food stamps and Medicaid coverage. I went into labor on the day right after I received my Medicaid card in the mail. At 17, I was very naive about my health and my body, and I was being "cared for" by my husband's very unethical general doctor. This so-called physician had never done a thorough exam (since he didn't even have a female nurse or assistant in the office). Early on, when I visited him with flu-like symptoms, he said I was pregnant based on his palpating my flat abdomen with my clothes on and stating, "Oh yes, she is definitely pregnant!" At that point, I was probably only six weeks pregnant, and I was a very petite 95-pound teen with a very flat belly. I wondered how he could tell I was pregnant, but I thought to myself, "Yes! My baby will be a big bouncing baby just like his 'Daddy' who had weighed 11lbs at birth!!"

The doctor said, "Oh no, if the baby is too big, you will need to have a C- section." He had now 'planted the seed' that the baby might be too large for a vaginal delivery. That doctor recommended we get on a payment plan towards a surgeon's fees for my C-section, since he was neither a surgeon nor an obstetrician. We could pay in cash in his office on each of my visits. My 'prenatal' care was nonexistent. He gave me some pills that I assumed were vitamins, but I never really found out what they were. Looking back, they were probably 'salt' pills because I blew up into a 180 lb. balloon on my 5ft frame by the time I went into labor. That summer, my feet were so swollen, I had to borrow my Papi's slippers to waddle around. The doctor had me get an X-ray a few weeks before my supposed due date. Somehow, he convinced us that my cervix could not give birth to my son, and he had us continue the payment plan for the C-section. On the morning of my son's birth, I woke up from a strange dream where viscous fluids were oozing out of my body and I woke up in a pool of "water". I called the doctor, and he said to meet him at the hospital. Before ending the call, he asked, "Do you have the balance of the Surgeon's payment?" I said, "No, but yesterday I received a Medicaid card..." He cut me off briskly and said, "Go to another hospital!" as he hung up on me. What the...? As I sat in my puddle of 'water', I had to think quickly. The day before, I had researched all available hospitals that accepted Medicaid and I asked my husband to take me to Misericordia Hospital in the North Bronx. I used a bunch of his t-shirts as pads to collect the 'water' that kept oozing out of me for our 15-minute drive.

The unscrupulous doctor was a general MD with ties to a local politician. Since he was neither an obstetrician nor a surgeon and could not perform surgery at the local hospital, I don't think Medicaid would reimburse for those "surgeon" fees. Back then, there were no electronic records and if he were to be audited, there would not be any record of vital signs or visits with a female nurse or other assistant. I never saw him writing notes, and he never checked my weight or blood pressure himself.

The nun/nurses at the hospital were very nurturing when I showed up in the ER. My heart was pounding as I told them, "My doctor said I needed a C-section!" I was so worried because I didn't know what would happen to my baby if I didn't have the C-section! My doctor would not answer calls from the nuns/nurses at the hospital I went to. They performed another set of X-rays to determine why I might need a C-section. Since the doctor would not answer their calls, they needed to determine why I would need a C-section if my son had hydrocephalus, for example. (I did not have a C-sect.) In the meantime, they took me to a room where they examined me, shaved me, and gave me an enema, as that was standard procedure in the 1970s. They did not allow anyone else in the room with me, not even my husband. I was so alone and cold in that sterile room. There was a slew of interns and nurses coming in sporadically to check my cervix (my first-ever pelvic exam) or take me to the bathroom. I only remember having the urge to move my bowels — no cramps. I was completely clueless and when I asked, "When will I have my C-section?" They laughed and looked at me like I had two heads! They got the rest of the 'team' to take me to the delivery room instead…All I remember after that was the staff telling me to push 'one more time' and I was pushing as if to have a final bowel movement and when I was about to yell, "I can't anymore!" They put a mask over my face and the next thing I remember is opening my eyes in a quiet setting and the nurse asking me to push so I could deliver the placenta and they were congratulating me on the birth of my boy. All I could say was, "Already?" since it felt like seconds when it had been hours. I had a healthy, bouncing 7lb, 4oz baby boy vaginally with the requisite episiotomy of the times and my first experience with hemorrhoids!

My husband was absent from the birth and marriage that first year. Supposedly, he had very long hours at his new job. He was always claiming to be at his mother's home for dinner, so I wouldn't have to cook for him. Unbeknown to me, he was already in another relationship with someone else. In the meantime, I confided in my best friend from HS, Corey, about my unhappy marriage. Corey tried to be supportive and even paid for us to learn Transcendental Meditation to help with my struggles, but all his caring and supportive ways made me fall in love with him instead.

In Spring 1973, when I was supposed to be preparing for an HS prom, I was instead, an 18yo, in my dark, dreary apartment (my husband had painted the living room walls black with an abstract drawing) washing cloth diapers for my baby and fixing formula in the galley kitchen. My husband would periodically broach the subject of separating for a 'little while' because he had not been a bachelor for long and I would always go into a panic and sob inconsolably. I'm sure he thought I was suicidal! But by Labor Day 1973, my son was a year old, and I was so into Corey that when my husband came to broach the subject of going away for the weekend for the umpteenth time, I no longer had a panic attack…instead, I said, "I think you are right. You should go away, but not just for the long weekend. Leave and do not come back!" He was speechless, and he left! I realized that my 'panic' was not about the loss of my love. My angst was about the thought of being a single teen mom without a job or a high school diploma and how to manage my finances and motherhood on my own.

I found out through an old school friend that she had asked him about our breakup. I told her we were too young to get married, and we just started growing apart. It was amicable. She said he had remarked that, at least, his new woman "cleaned and cooked" for him! I felt like I had just been sucker punched in the gut! I didn't even know there was another woman and then to be informed by my school friend was just too humiliating! I had learned to cook well during that year, but he kept telling me not to cook because he would eat at his mother's home, or that he was in the (non-existent) 'bowling league'. I had turned into a regular 'Susie homemaker' that year. I had to keep the small apartment immaculate, as he would lift the lamps up to make sure I had not missed a spot. I also had to wash the cloth diapers daily since my son was allergic to the new, disposable Pampers! The entire apartment usually smelled like bleach since I had to keep them sanitized.

I had to figure out how to fend for myself and my baby without a job or education. Why didn't I listen to Mami? He had also told a mutual friend of ours that if he found out that I got a job, he would not help me out financially!

That friend, who was the wife of his best friend, put in a good word for me at Chemical Bank and arranged for me to have an interview. At the interview, I took a skills test, and I aced the memory section. I could start work, making $75 a week on my own! It was through that job that I would get my GED, eventually. I couldn't survive on that low pay, though. I had to pay rent and buy food and supplies for my child. In the meantime, true to his word, for once, my husband went 'MIA'. My landlord convinced me to apply for public assistance, which was very taboo for me. Papi had always worked two or three jobs so that Mami could stay at home with us and not have to go 'on welfare'! With a letter from my landlord, I could receive partial assistance to help with food stamps and health coverage for my baby. And here's where I stumbled and had to get right up and keep on keeping on.

Working at Chemical Bank began around the end of 1973. I needed to apply for 'partial' public assistance or a subsidy, and I remember going to the city office in my 'business' clothes. While in the waiting area, I sat next to a Caucasian woman who was making small talk and said, "That's right, honey. You shouldn't be ashamed to get help, too, if all of them can get it!" as she smirked, looking at all the other women of color waiting for their turn at an interview. I kept quiet and let her ramble on when she asked, "What are you, Sweetie?" I calmly said, "Puerto Rican" with a smile, and the woman's face turned beet red and without another word, she turned and walked away. You see, my phenotype is fair-skinned with freckles and my English is quite articulate, although I can also speak fluent Spanish and "Spanglish" if needed. I have been mistaken for Italian, Spanish, Russian, or Jewish in the past. It wasn't the first time nor the last time that I would have such a bigoted response from someone. I let it wash over me like water off a duck's back since I looked at this partial assistance as a 'bridge' loan until I could make it on my own. This was not a permanent situation.

At work, I had no perception of moving up in the corporate world or that there was even a hierarchy. I was just so grateful to have a job and I was very diligent with my filing tasks in the back offices. Both Papi and Mami have always instilled a work ethic in me that 'whatever you do, do your best.'

I was fortunate to live near my parents at the time and Mami was more than willing to help care for my boy while I worked. At 18, I was so naïve about the "business" world. The only work clothes I had were my skimpy dresses and heels (I have always been a girly girl) which I wore to my job in the back office of Chemical Bank on Park Ave. On my way to work one day, a strange man stopped and said, "Wait, wait! Don't tell me, everyone tells you, you look just like Bette Midler, right?" After I had my son, I kept a little weight in all the right places. I wasn't sure if he meant it as a compliment or just an observation. I still don't know how I could commute from the Bronx into Midtown Manhattan, work a full 8-hour day, and travel back home daily in my spiked heels.

I was so grateful to have a job that I would have cleaned the toilet if they asked me to. They did not. My responsibilities included filing and accessing files in one of their trust areas, and I couldn't understand why the much older women who had worked there for 20 years or more did not seem to like me. The seasoned and complacent workers didn't seem to appreciate my enthusiasm. It made them look bad; I suppose. I developed a rapport with one VP in the trust office because I anticipated which files she would need, and would always have them ready. Thanks to her, I advanced to another department in the bank where I received training on using the microfiche machine and retrieving archived files. I was more independent there, and I didn't have to deal with the snickering older workers anymore. While there, they gave me the opportunity to take evening classes in lower Manhattan to prepare for my GED. Around that time, I also read about creative visualization and how the mind doesn't distinguish your thoughts between reality and fantasy, so I began doing my own visualizing. I was told that any score near 300 on the GED exam was a good score and I didn't want to seem too presumptuous, so I visualized "299". I got 296 and then I became more specific with my visualizations - lesson learned. My lesson was to not fear dreaming big! I have since successfully used visualization many times, particularly in my career, preparing for interviews and job offers, for example.

All right now, let us delve into the beginnings of my journey of obstacles…

"The struggle you're in today is developing the strength you need tomorrow."

Robert Tew

Chapter Two

"Don't be pushed around by the fears in your mind. Be led by the dreams in your heart."

Roy T. Bennett

Numbers, Naiveté, and Navigating New Beginnings

Hi there! Let's dive into the next chapter of my wild and unpredictable journey. Picture this: a young, naive version of me, filled with dreams, hopes, and a passion for numbers that would shape the course of my life. Let's go!

As far back as I can remember, I've always had this thing for puzzles and numbers. Even when I was just a little kid in elementary school, math and science were my thing. While other kids were playing after school, I was doing extra homework for math and science classes until late evenings. Yeah, I was a nerd. It's funny how those early interests can end up defining your path in life, isn't it?

I'll never forget what Mami used to tell me. When I was just a tiny tot of six months old, she and my older sister would say, "Iris, cuenta, Iris" (which means "Iris, count, Iris" in Spanish). And guess what? Little me, lying in my crib, would blurt out, "Uno, dos, tres, cuatro, cinco... diez!" Yep, I was a math prodigy in the making, even if I was small for my age, and that made it even funnier for them. My family always found joy in my early numerical prowess, and it became one of those little quirks that defined me.

That love for numbers and puzzles has stuck with me throughout the years. Whenever I face challenges or problems, it's like my brain turns into a puzzle-solving machine. It starts working on its own, rearranging thoughts, shifting things around, and somehow finding the perfect solution at just the right time. It is like my brain is wired differently; you know? It's a gift that has both fascinated and served me well, guiding me through the labyrinth of life.

But let me take you back to a pivotal moment in my life—a moment that would set the stage for the trials and triumphs that lay ahead. Imagine this: I was 18, a young single mom, trying to navigate the complexities of adulthood while raising my precious child. The yearning for stability and security tugged at my heart, but little did I know that a storm was brewing on the horizon.

At the time, I was married to a man who was desperate to bail on our marriage before we even hit our second anniversary. Can you imagine the panic and fear that set in? I was terrified of being left alone to raise my child without a job or even a high school diploma. It was an emotional rollercoaster, to say the least.

You know, looking back, I realize just how naive I was as a teenager. I thought I had it all figured out. I mean, I lucked out with this guy, right? He was supposed to take care of me, so who needs a career? Papi had always been a great provider, so I thought lightning would strike twice. Boy was I wrong.

There were so many red flags I missed with him. Looking back, it's as clear as day. Even his mother warned me on our wedding day, saying, "Oh, you know what a liar he is..." I remember being offended, thinking, how can a mother say that about her own son? But now, older and wiser, I realize she knew him better than anyone. Mothers have an uncanny ability to see through the fallacies we sometimes fall for.

Once our son was born, things started unraveling at an alarming rate. My husband became distant, and his family seemed disinterested in our little bundle of joy. Turns out, he wasn't ready for the responsibilities of fatherhood or, frankly, for being a decent human being. He disappeared one day, leaving nothing but shattered dreams and unpaid bills in his wake. There I was, holding the pieces of a broken home, desperately searching for a way to put them back together.

My heart sank. I felt like I had failed as a wife and as a mother. But I knew I couldn't let that define me. My son deserved better, and I needed to step up and be the rock he could rely on. So, with my little boy in one arm and determination in the other, I set out to rebuild our lives from scratch.

Thankfully, there was a ray of light in my life during those tough times. My best friend from HS, Corey, was my rock. We were like two peas in a pod. When he came home on breaks from college, he stayed with me, even helping financially. He was caring, compassionate, and supportive. I couldn't have asked for a better friend. Ah, those were memorable days.

Looking back, I often wonder how different things could have been if I had not let him go for selfish reasons. Love can be a tricky thing, huh? Life has a way of playing out as it must, and sometimes we just have to live with the choices we've made.

First things first: I needed an income. As I mentioned before, I started an entry-level position in a bank even though I did not have an HS diploma. I had to apply for public assistance because I didn't make enough money to pay rent and provide food and healthcare for my boy. Education was the key to unlocking a better future, not just for me but for my son, too, so I enrolled in a local adult education program, determined to overcome the obstacles that stood between me and that piece of paper. Picture this: a young, single mom, juggling parenthood, a full-time job, and late-night study sessions. It was rough. Really rough.

But you know what? I had a fire burning inside me— a fire fueled by the love I had for my son and the burning desire to prove everyone wrong. I wasn't just going to get that diploma; I was going to make sure it was my stepping stone to a brighter future. Failure was not an option.

Finally, after what felt like an eternity, the day of the big exam arrived. My hands trembled as I held that pencil, staring at the intimidating rows of questions. Doubts crept into my mind, whispering, "What if you're not good enough? What if you've wasted all this time?" But I shut those voices out, reminding myself of all the hurdles I had already overcome. I closed my eyes and visualized getting my passing results as if it were that very moment. I then took a long deep breath and began.

I poured my heart and soul into that test, leaving no question unanswered. And when I finally put that pencil down, a mix of exhaustion and relief washed over me. I had done it. I had conquered that mountain, and the victory was sweet.

A few weeks later, (remember it was 1975 with snail mail) I received the news I had been waiting for. I passed! The joy that surged through me was indescribable. It was validation—the proof that I could achieve greatness, even in the face of adversity. I clutched that diploma in my hands, tears streaming down my face. It represented so much more than a piece of paper; it symbolized resilience, determination, and a brighter future.

But my journey was far from over. That diploma was just the beginning—a gateway to new opportunities and challenges that awaited me in the halls of higher education. College? Me? The idea seemed like a far-fetched dream. Private schools weren't known for accepting students like me, with just a GED. But you know what? I decided to give it a shot. After all, what did I have to lose?

To my surprise, the doors of opportunity swung wide open. Long Island University (LIU)-Brooklyn campus, a private school, accepted me. Can you believe it? Suddenly, a whole new world of possibilities opened before my eyes. It was like stepping into a parallel universe, where dreams could come true, even for a young single mom like me. I saw a chance to become a professional nurse, to make a decent living for my son and me. It meant investing four more years of my life, but the thought of no longer depending on public assistance or my deadbeat ex-husband for child support fueled my determination. There was light at the end of the tunnel, and I was only a couple of years "behind" schedule.

Now, let me tell you, the thought of going to college was equal parts exhilarating and terrifying. There I was, a woman in her twenties, walking into lecture halls filled with fresh-faced teenagers. I felt a pang of self-consciousness at first, questioning whether I belonged there. But as time went on, I realized that age was just a number, and my life experiences gave me a unique perspective that enriched my learning journey.

College life was a whirlwind of late-night study sessions, mind-boggling assignments, and coffee-fueled cramming sessions. I immersed myself in the world of study once again, pursuing a degree in nursing. And you know what? It felt like coming home. The intricacies of science and math—it all clicked into place.

But college wasn't just about academics. It was a melting pot of cultures, ideas, and friendships. I met incredible individuals from all walks of life, each with their own story to tell. We supported each other through the highs and lows, forming bonds that would last a lifetime. More about those years coming up.

So, there you have it—my journey from a young, naive girl fascinated by numbers to a determined single mom, overcoming obstacles and chasing her dreams. It hasn't always been easy, and there have been plenty of ups and downs along the way. But you know what? I wouldn't change a thing. Every twist and turn, every triumph and setback, has shaped me into the person I am today.

Now, as I sit here, reflecting on my journey, I can't help but smile. Life has a funny way of leading us down unexpected paths, doesn't it? But I've learned to embrace the uncertainties, to trust in my own abilities, and to believe in the power of dreams. And who knows what lies ahead? The adventure continues, and I can't wait to see where the numbers and my unwavering determination will take me next.

So, whether you're on the brink of a new beginning or knee-deep in the throes of your own adventure, remember this: embrace your passions, face your fears head-on, and never underestimate the power of your dreams. You never know where they might lead you.

Stay tuned for the next chapter, where I'll share more about my journey through college and the triumphs and trials that awaited me. Life's an adventure, dear reader.

Until next time, keep chasing those dreams and always believe in yourself. Cheers to new beginnings

Chapter Three

"As you start to walk on the way,
the way appears."

Rumi

Higher Education as a Single Mom

Dear reader, this is the first part of my journey to get back on track as a single mom pursuing higher education. My first year as a returning student started with so much momentum! I enrolled in a sociology course, and I wrote a paper that I was incredibly proud of. It took some serious legwork because, back in 1975, there was no Internet or readily available copy machines. I had to physically go to Hunter College in Manhattan, where they had an extensive collection of literature on Puerto Rican studies in their library. Today, it's known as the Center for Puerto Rican Studies, which collaborated with the African Studies program in the 1970s to become a division of the City University of NY (CUNY).

Through my research, I discovered a different perspective on Puerto Rican history, one that wasn't the usual "colonized" version. I learned that the word "taíno" was what the native Arawak people said when Columbus arrived. It meant "good," as in "hey, we've got visitors!" Columbus mistakenly called them "Taíno Indians," as he thought he had reached India instead of the Western world. I delved into the blending of three cultures - the European colonizers, the indigenous natives, and the enslaved Africans brought over for labor when the native population was almost wiped out. In my paper, I explored how this blending manifested in our modern-day Puerto Rican (Boricua) culture, particularly in the common language of music, as evident in the rural areas, "bomba." Even today, the beat of the congas and the sight of dancers in their old-world white dresses move me deeply. I was incredibly proud of that term paper, even though I had only one copy since I typed it out on an old typewriter.

Unfortunately, my overall grade in the course wasn't as good as I had hoped, primarily because the instructor turned out to be a predator. Initially, He impressed me, despite his physical appearance resembling a slightly tall dwarf. He had an air of arrogance and a pompous attitude that tricked me into thinking he was someone to impress. He asked me and another attractive young woman to discuss our essays individually and privately in his office, implying that we could become his "friends." Little did I know what he truly meant.

During our meeting, he shared details about his life and where he lived, near prominent political figures in Westchester, New York. Then, out of nowhere, he inched his chair closer to me and made a horrifying statement while fondling my breasts with his stubby fingers. He said, "If anything were to happen between us, no one would ever believe you since I am the Chair of the department, and who would you have to complain to?" The fear paralyzed me. I had to get out of there, but I had no idea how to finish the course. I don't even remember how the meeting ended, but I knew I would never step foot in his office again. I didn't need his so-called "friendship" if that's what it meant. I managed to escape that situation, dodging a bullet. He gave me an A+ for the paper, but I only received a C for the overall class. It turned out he accused me of cheating because a few of us, in a study group, had the same answers in the final exam, while the male students, with the same answers, received A's. If only I had known then what I know now, I would have reported him to someone at LIU, the state education authorities, or even the police. But back then, I was just relieved to have completed the class and never see him again.

Wow, that first year at LIU was a rollercoaster ride! I wanted to explore all the liberal arts courses before settling on a major. So, I took a drama class and ended up acting in a play. Can you believe it? Balancing rehearsals, classes, and being a mom to a toddler was no joke, but oh boy, it was such an exhilarating time in my life! I was lucky enough to have fellow student friends who were willing to pick up my son from daycare on late rehearsal nights.

They had this adaptation of "12 Angry Men" called "12 Angry People," and guess what? I landed a role as a Cuban refugee juror, complete with Mami's accent. I nailed it! I impressed everybody. One day, this drama major even called me a 'natural.' Can you imagine? For a second, I thought I could be the next big thing in acting, you know? Getting discovered and all! But reality hit me like a ton of bricks.

So, this other director discovered me and cast me in a second play. The catch was it was a role I wasn't familiar with—I had to play an old maid. They powdered my hair and added a few wrinkles with some fancy makeup. Bam! I was suddenly forty years older. The director thought I was some accent specialist, so he had me audition with a British accent. He kept saying, "Make it less classy." What did he mean? The director even gave me tapes to practice with. But try as I might, I couldn't get the cockney accent he wanted right. It was a struggle. And guess what? The reviews for that play weren't great. That's when it hit me—I needed to stick to my original plan.

You know, the Spanish accent in the first play came naturally to me because I grew up with Spanish-speaking parents and English is not my first language. At the performances, people who didn't know me thought I was not fluent in English. But when it comes to British accents, forget it! I'd only seen those on TV, and let's be honest, I didn't have a clue.

Another extracurricular activity I was very interested in at LIU was gymnastics.

Back in the1960s, when I was a tween, physical education wasn't a big thing for me. I went to a Roman Catholic school without a gym in the middle of 144th St. Recess? That happened on the street after they closed it off to traffic. I was too busy being nerdy and studious to have many friends or get much exercise. But then came high school at Bronx High School of Science, and they made us take Physical Ed every year. And you know what? I loved it! I even played basketball. I had dreams of doing gymnastics, but it felt like an impossible dream. Those gymnasts at my high school had special training at these schools called 'Sokols' in New Jersey, and they had all these fancy outfits and stuff. Meanwhile, I had never even heard of these Sokols in the South Bronx.

Fast forward to 1975, and I found myself spending a lot of time with my brother's gymnastics team at LIU. I even managed the rehearsals for the female gymnastics team. Can you believe it? At twenty, I was learning cartwheels! It was something I had always been interested in, but growing up in the South Bronx projects, it seemed out of reach. But being around those gymnasts was so inspiring.

During my time at LIU, I re-discovered the joy of dancing, too. My weekends were 'free' because Mami was more than willing to spend time with my boy. Every Friday night, there were these epic parties in the main building. Picture this—a former theater-turned-dance floor with no chairs, just open space to boogie down. It was the disco era, and boy, did I love doing the hustle. It was like salsa dancing, and I had been dancing salsa since I was a baby. Mami used to say I was dancing before I could even walk. At six months old, I would stand in the crib and the adults would have to hold my tiny hands so I could 'dance' to the Latin beats! Back in 1975 at LIU, there I was, going to these parties and dancing my heart out. I even had my eye on this one guy who had some smooth moves, but he was way too full of himself to notice me. Typical, right?

But you know who came to my rescue? My brother's best friend from the gymnastics team. As soon as "Rock the Boat" by Hues Corp started playing, he asked me to dance, and we were like Fred Astaire and Ginger Rogers, just gliding across the floor. He was such a gentleman, and dancing with him was pure magic. We became lifelong friends, even though we haven't seen each other since Mami's memorial in 2013. Whenever I hear "Rock the Boat" or "Do the Hustle" by Van McCoy or Donna Summer's "Last Dance," it takes me right back to those incredible dancing days. Even now, I can't help but move to the music, whether I have a dance partner or not.

Ah, those were the days! LIU was a time of exploration, growth, and unforgettable experiences. I dabbled in acting, found a love for physical education and dance, and ultimately solidified my path toward a healthcare career. Those years shaped me and taught me some valuable lessons. Like, always make copies of your work, and never underestimate the power of a good dance partner. As I step into my next creative endeavors, I'll always remember those lessons and keep the spirit of dance alive in my heart. Next, I'll delve into more of my new beginnings in Brooklyn...

Chapter Four

"The wound is the place where the
Light enters you."

Rumi

Brooklyn years 1975-1978

Okay before classes began in September 1975, I needed to do a little research about where I would live in Brooklyn, I researched apartments near LIU, as traveling from the Bronx daily was quite challenging. I found an apartment in a three-family house across from an elementary school which was within walking distance to LIU. I also found a daycare center which had recently opened in 1970 by the House of the Lord Church. Today it's called Alonzo A Daughtry Memorial Day Care Center and still exists. The center was available from 8:00 AM to 6:00 PM, which was great for me, and I could stagger my classes. Sometimes I could go home for lunch for a bit before going back to my classes. I already told you how my four-year-old son reacted to our move to Brooklyn in 1975. In the Bronx, Mami had spoiled him so much. He was also a very picky eater and Mami would feed him anything his little heart desired. His day care center had structure and healthy veggies for snacks, and scheduled nap times during the day. The first few weeks were particularly trying. At home, I tried cooking meals I knew he liked, but he was also refusing to eat any of them, even when I tried negotiating with him. I tried reasoning with him by letting him know that I didn't expect him to like everything, but he had to, at least, try different things, and then, if he didn't like them, he wouldn't have to eat them. It took several weeks, but eventually, he came around. He never took naps, though. Once he told me that naps were "wasting time". I often wonder if my son's behavior then would be diagnosed as attention deficit disorder today.

The first year at LIU was liberating me from my old struggles of the past two years. My new beginnings included traveling to Brooklyn and taking multiple liberal arts courses. I already told you about my debacle with my acting aspirations. After that drama (pun intended) gave me a reality check, I chose to major in Respiratory Therapy, at the recommendation of a not-so-loyal 'friend' and they accepted me into the track when the "Tsunami" hit...

At the end of 1975, we moved into the second floor of the house across from a public school in Brooklyn. The first floor was for the 'Super's' family of six children and the third floor was rented out to two soccer players who attended LIU. I made friends easily at LIU and most of my friends were male. I had one female (so-called friend) who often visited. Often, I would hang out in my apartment with one of my male friends, who always confided his sexual escapades to me when we smoked pot during lunch hours. It was a very convenient hangout since it was so close to the campus. Since I had daycare for most of the day, I had work-study for financial aid. Another female friend and I were the first females allowed to work as painters, mainly at the dorms on-site. The pay was more than for the office positions, which made them more alluring. She and I were so detail-oriented that they began hiring more females on the painting sites. The males were very complacent and didn't seem to take pride in their work. My friend and I were thrilled with the extra income. We even started offering our services, and that's how I met a coach and I offered to paint the locker rooms for a set fee. I physically became involved with this older married man. I had never been in such a relationship before. When I witnessed this beautiful and very pregnant woman walk up to greet him one afternoon, I could not, in good conscience, keep seeing him. This was not one of my finer moments.

Meanwhile, on the home front, I didn't realize that the neighbor downstairs had a reputation as the town gossip, and she viewed me as some kind of 'Jezebel' bringing in men to the house. She played bingo with the other stay-at-home moms in the neighborhood, and she was on public assistance even though all the children were already in school across the street. From my window, I could see the dad (the super) come over during recess and play with them in our backyard and I would have such guilty feelings about being such an inadequate mom. I have always been very 'girly' and academic and not sports-minded at all. I was depriving my son of a wholesome boyhood because he did not have a father figure. I knew very little about sports. In those days, I felt like I had failed him. But I am not the one who left my son. His father did not take any interest in his life at all.

One day, while I was sitting on the stoop after school, I got into an argument with the two soccer players from the third floor. I don't even remember what we were arguing about and the "super" dad, "L-" came to the stoop and tried to 'diffuse' the situation and told us that we were "educated" students, but we were not behaving that way. When the two soccer players went upstairs, L- stayed there, talking to me in a very paternal manner (he was 15 years my senior). He said, "It doesn't look good that you keep bringing different boys to your home every day." He said I was getting a bad reputation with the women on that street, especially the one downstairs (Baby Mama). After his 'lecture', L- made me promise to stop that behavior.

The next day he met up with me on the way back from school and before I got to the building (alone). He brought me a little "present" and it was a small pewter fishing lure. He said, "Since we are both Pisces, I brought this over for you." "I was going to have it gold-filled but then I just decided to give it to you today." I can't believe I fell for that nonsense! Really? Then again, I had never been fishing and would not know what a pewter fishing lure was, anyway. Somehow in the conversations, he led me to believe that he was the super of the building but was not living with the mother and children. I don't even remember what else we spoke about, but when I got upstairs, one of my female friends was already there with my son and this overwhelming emotion came over me that, to this day, I can't explain! When she saw my pale face and teary eyes, she said, "What's wrong?" I couldn't speak. I just began sobbing uncontrollably, and I didn't know why. I stopped for a bit to call Mami, and said, "Mami pray for me. I think I found the one...!" Who says, "Pray for me!' when announcing good news? I could not explain then or now why I was crying. I simply resumed sobbing the rest of the night.

I still cannot tell if the emotion was happy, sad, miserable, or elation... It was just such a kaleidoscope of emotions that, reflecting on it, I feel it was the Universe supernaturally guiding me towards my fate. I cannot say that I had strong emotions for L-. It's not like there was any chemistry there. He was much older than me and he was balding, and he was missing teeth. I have seen pictures of him in his youth and he was handsome, but not when I met him. Sometimes I just feel Spirit was guiding me to be a 'sacrificial lamb'. I genuinely believe that we choose how we want to come into this world and my child has chosen! I had to meet him so that my daughter could be born, and she could be who she is.

From 1976-1977 is a bit of a blur and I remember bits and pieces of it. Selective memory, I guess. L- had me meet him at other apartments that he supposedly had access to as a superintendent, and I don't remember how, but we became physical. I know he introduced me to porno videos to teach me all about oral sex. I also remember that he was quite rough, not sweet, and tender. He was very controlling and slowly started 'liquidating' my past. I had a collection of Papi's coins specifically, copper pennies and silver dimes that L- "borrowed" but I never saw again. I also had a unique wooden sculpture that Corey had made for me, and L- got jealous and threw it away. At some point and I don't remember the timeline, by early 1977, the Baby Mama situation got really dark with her coming up to my door with a hammer or machete and I don't remember how I escaped with my son and went to Mami's in the Bronx until L- found an apartment in a five-floor walkup in the Bronx. He had the keys to my apartment in Brooklyn and while I was in the Bronx, he 'sold' my treasured bike that Corey had given me, too.

On July 13, 1977. I was in the 5-floor walk-up Bronx apartment without a phone or furniture during the New York City blackout that lasted 36 hours! L- had brought over a Doberman Pinscher, his favorite kind of dog, named "Dillinger". Why? I don't even know where this dog came from. L- went to Brooklyn to celebrate one of his daughter's birthdays and left us in that dark apartment. There I was with my son and a not-so-friendly dog when all the lights went out! I did not have a clue what was going on and we didn't yet have a telephone, so there was no way to communicate with anyone. All I remember from that night was seeing white, growling teeth in the darkness. "Dillinger" must have been picking up my anxiety. Well, somehow, I survived those hours. Little did I know, I was already pregnant with my second child.

Fall, 1977: It's never the right time for a pregnancy, but this was clearly the worst. I was back on track with my career and education and now I would have to take steps back again. I had seriously considered ending the pregnancy, and I told L-. He agreed and even went with me to a clinic, but when we got there, I froze. I could not even walk to the intake desk. I slowly turned toward the exit and looked at him and he just had this big smile. So, we walked out and never spoke of a termination again. For his part, he was elated to contribute another 'seed' into the world. By my count, this would be his eighth offspring, as his first was living in Puerto Rico with his mom, or so I thought.

That Bronx apartment was a short stay, and he next found an apartment back in Brooklyn since I was still at LIU. It was not as close to the school, and I had to take the "G" train to get to school. Who knew there was a "G" train? I was still taking liberal arts courses and had begun voice lessons. L- would time how long it would take from my last class to get home and was getting paranoid about my "relationship" with my professor, since the lessons were individual. My professor felt I had real potential for professional singing, but I could not concentrate as I had to ensure I didn't miss my train home. I don't know how I completed that class with all the stress.

At the Brooklyn apartment, he began bringing four or five of the six kids over regularly. I only had food stamps for my boy and me, but here I was sharing whatever I had with his kids, even though they all had plenty of food stamps for the entire brood. Baby Mama didn't seem to mind getting her kids out of her own hands if it was with me with my food stamps. The children were also under a lot of stress and one day L- started up an argument with me for no reason at all he put a knife to my throat in their presence, traumatizing them, as they knew I was pregnant, and they grew up with these episodes between him and their mom. I knew he was just putting on an act for them. I did not fear him back then.

He was quite the "drama queen". Every time he became irrational, his eyes bulged, and he looked 'crazy'. One day he brought home handcuffs, and he attached himself to the radiator (we were on the third floor) he gave me the key and said, "No matter how much I beg, don't unlock them until tomorrow morning!! OK?" I did just that and after a few hours, he started his histrionics. One minute he would ask sweetly and the next his eyes would bulge, and his demeanor almost looked diabolical as he cried and demanded to be freed. I just looked at him and said, "No, you said not to, no matter what you say!" I left him there, sitting on the floor and connected to the radiator, even when he lifted the radiator about a foot off the ground. That old radiator connected to the floor below us! It was a long night, but there were no consequences the next morning.

He wasn't just irrational with me... One day after I was already home, I heard a commotion outside the door with some teens. I cracked open the door to see they were threatening him and saying they knew who his "wife" was and that they could hurt me, too. The next thing I heard in a high-pitched voice saying, "Aah, aahh!" and I then witnessed him lifting his arms and one leg as if he were going to do some martial arts like the Karate Kid and the gang just laughed at him so hard and mimicked him before they left. They never approached me. I'm not sure how I survived those months and still succeeded in my classes until February 1978. That was the last semester I attended LIU, before the birth of my Light.

March 1978. After the semester was over in February, I stayed in the Bronx at Mami and Papi's home so I could be closer to the hospital in the Bronx. My son could not be more pleased to be living at 'Mama's' again and going back to his old ways with behaviors and eating. My due date was the beginning of March and I needed to feel supported and not abandoned in Brooklyn with L-'s erratic behavior. I also wanted to be as peaceful as possible and not project any negative energy onto my unborn child. I did the best I could, but I think my precious gem still had some of that negative energy embedded in her psyche. In any case, I was now under the care of a new obstetrician who worked with a Nurse Practitioner. I was not interested in finding out the baby's gender. I just wanted to have a healthy baby. I also wanted to have a natural childbirth. They were very supportive at this hospital.

This time around, I was more knowledgeable, and I would not be swindled by an unscrupulous doctor, like with my first pregnancy. I began feeling these "butterfly" sensations near my left hip around my birthday and I thought I would have my baby early. After all, my son was born two weeks before his due date. They were just Braxton-Hicks contractions. I got them for L-'s birthday too, but I was told I would not have the baby for another two weeks. Back then I was fit, and I didn't have the usual pregnancy issues during this one, but I was tired of being pregnant and ready to meet my little bundle of joy that I had been bonding with for the past nine months! I had a scheduled appointment on Good Friday expecting to hear that I would have my baby by the end of the day and one of the staff told bet that I would have the baby on Easter (Resurrection) Sunday. It's a good thing I am not a betting person! I would have lost that one.

On March 26, 1978, at 3:37 PM, Resurrection Sunday, I gave birth to a seven pound, eight-ounce baby girl. I had her by natural childbirth with my Nurse Practitioner present and L- was there. As soon as she was born, they placed her on my belly, and she suckled as if it were her last meal. They had to break the suction with a finger to get her cleaned up. They let L- hold her briefly, and he said the stupidest thing ever, as he pretended to tap her little bum, he said, "This is for all the trouble you've put us through!" WTF! "Trouble"? I kid you not, my precious baby girl, made this funny little noise like, "Huh, huh" or like "Oh, this is the part where I cry?" My baby never cried. It is said that a mom can recognize her child's cry anywhere. Well, not this mom! I doubt I could ever recognize her cries, as she never cried. We were both in sync with our rest and eating times. My baby would sleep and after I ate, she would make that little "huh, huh" sound, and I knew she was ready to nurse. Every time I nursed her, the most euphoric feeling would come over me when I cradled my baby in my arms to feed her. I suppose it was oxytocin, the "love" hormone. I always felt like nothing in the world could disrupt this most exquisite, serene moment.

I named her Taína after our ancestors from Puerto Rico. Taíno means good. Throughout the pregnancy, I could not think of a boy's name even though I was sure that I was having a boy. I had this name, Taína, (the feminine of taíno in Spanish) in my head the whole time. The name fits my daughter perfectly, and she has the cinnamon-colored skin of the indigenous people of our ancestors. I wanted to honor that part of my ancestry. My titi Flor, Mami's older sister, did not approve of that name. She said it represented a weak people that were conquered and 'annihilated'. This isn't true. Many taíno retreated to the more mountainous areas of the island and the (Spanish) colonizers stopped documenting their status on census forms, so it appears that there were no more "Indians", only black, white, and mulattos. The indigenous people of the island were written out of existence by the colonizers. Since I am 27% Indigenous Puerto Rican according to my DNA testing, I know that part of me has not been annihilated.

Taína was born with a pear-shaped beauty mark on her lower back, and I found it amusing because I ate a lot of pears during this pregnancy. She also has a beauty mark over her knuckles where there had been a scab from her sucking on her fist in the womb. Taína says she thinks she was born ready to fight for me. She is still very assertive as an adult.

I used to sing "The most beautiful sound I ever heard..." to the tune of the West Side Story song, but I substituted 'Taína' for 'Maria'. I still put that in any correspondence I send her. I truly believe that my girl was born on Resurrection Sunday for a reason. During the pregnancy, I returned to my love of crocheting which my older sister had taught me as a child. I crocheted a baby blanket with the pastel colors of pink, blue, and yellow since I didn't know what I would have. My baby had that blanket for years into her teen years when she was living at Mami's. Taína truly has been a light and blessing to me, and since she chose me to be her mom, that is why I had that tempest of her father in my life.

Stay tuned for my 'happily ever after' - NOT.

Chapter Five

"Listen to your heart and trust the direction you are being pulled. Something inside you already knows what to do."

Spring Washam

Escape from NY

O kay, so after the birth of my second child, we moved back to Brooklyn. On a bright and sunny June day, I traveled with my 3-month-old daughter and my 5-year-old boy to the Bronx so that Mami could give me cash to pay our phone bill in Brooklyn. L- was not helping financially. Mami was willing to pay so that we could stay in communication, so we needed a landline for that. While I was visiting Mami on the Grand Concourse, she could spend a little time with my children as well. I had to go to Fordham Rd to pay the bill. I could take the bus from right in front of Mami's building or just walk and it was such a lovely day that I proceeded to walk to and from Fordham Rd. I wanted to stop off at a local shoe store on the way back, to buy little sandals for my baby. I was on the west side of the Concourse walking south back to Mami's when I heard him yelling obscenities at me. "I'll kill you! You lying B----!" Apparently, I had told him I was taking the bus to Fordham Rd but, instead I was walking on the Grand Concourse. He was yelling from the east side of the Concourse as he walked across the avenue to me. The Grand Concourse was wide, with total eight lanes running north and south through the Bronx and resembling an avenue in France... I thought, "I've got to get to the pizzeria!" because the police always hung out there and they knew me from the past seven years living in the neighborhood. I felt safe there, and I knew he would not go in because he was such a "chicken". He was that kind of coward, that only preyed on the defenseless. "This is the last straw!!" I just could not tolerate this behavior and bring up my children with this constant fear. As soon as I felt the coast was clear, I scrambled south on the east side of the Concourse with my heart pounding in my chest, straight to my parents' building. As soon as I walked in through the door, on the second floor, I said, "Mami, can I have money for a ticket to New Haven right now?" In about half an hour, I took my two children with the clothes we had on and my baby's diapers and took a cab to 125th St to the Metro North station. Destination - New Haven CT. It must have been the afternoon rush hour since all I saw on the train were mostly business suits and briefcases on this train. I had a blanket over my shoulder so I could breastfeed my baby all the way to New Haven. I'm not proud of it, but somehow, I felt my new 'broken' relationship was my five-year-old son's fault and I kept asking him, "Are you happy now?" as if he had orchestrated this whole scenario. I was feeling defeated as now I had two small children with different fathers and no good means to support them. This is how I wound up in New Haven, CT where my older sister lived with her five children.

"If you need to come to New Haven with your children, you are welcome to come as long as you leave that man." My sister's words had been playing in my head in between his tirade on the Concourse.

I left everything behind. We moved into her duplex just outside of the New Haven station until I found an apartment where I had assistance with heating oil. My sister gave me enough money to navigate transportation to find some temporary work and my young nieces would babysit for me. I had to wean my baby girl too soon. School was out for the summer and my sister was working for the city of New Haven. I found a temp position in the local white pages factory as a clerk for a couple of weeks and I also applied for public assistance in New Haven, which was so different from the New York experience. There, they treated me with respect, almost like I was at a job interview. The offices were clean, too. I did not want to be a burden to my sis, so I gave all my food stamps and stipend to her while I looked for my place. I kept enough for Taina's formula and diapers.

By the end of the summer of 1978, I'm not sure how, but my "baby daddy" found me and convinced me that he was a changed man and that he now worked as a truck driver and could help financially. I am not one to look back once I've decided, so even though it was out of character for me, I gave him a second chance. This time, I let him move into my new apartment as long as he knew that he would have no say in how to raise my son. This was short-lived and as soon as he moved in, he did have a job, but his behavior did not really change. Another stipulation about his moving back in with me would be that he could visit his other children in Brooklyn as much as he wanted if he did not bring them to New Haven. When we lived in Brooklyn, I had become a free babysitter for his other children.

Well, one evening as I looked out my window, there he was with four of the six children coming out of his 'circus' car! My body immediately reacted with intractable vomiting. We all wound up in the ER with all kinds of testing... When they suggested a 'barium swallow' test, I declined and told them I knew there was nothing physically wrong with me. I asked for a mental health referral instead. He didn't bring back the children except for one day when he went to visit them and he came back with his youngest son, who was about seven or eight. He claimed the boy had a day off from school, but he did not bring any clothes with the little one. He taught the little boy to go and hide in the 'dumbwaiter' in the middle of the house and wait for him to get back from work. He went to work, and a couple of hours later, the police or FBI (I'm not sure) were at my door with the boy's mom. They told me that if I did not turn over the boy, they would consider me an accomplice and they would charge me with kidnapping. This is before the days of 'amber alerts. I went to the dumbwaiter, and I told the boy to come out and go home with his mom.

I had begun attending a support group for domestic violence at the local YMCA. I was amazed by so many women who were abused physically and emotionally and were not sure what it was that they wanted out of their relationship. I knew in my heart that I wanted to get out of this situation, but he was always threatening to hurt my parents. I went home determined that whatever the next situation was, he would be out no matter what. I could not return to school while he was still in the picture.

From the first time I applied for partial public assistance, I knew I would use public help as a bridge to my end goal of having a career and being self-sustaining. Many people use the system to "get over" and they feed into the stereotypes that exist. I was determined to stop that cycle for myself, so before my baby was a year old, I decided I wanted to have a tubal ligation as permanent birth control. I had been asking my health providers what I needed to do to get a tubal ligation. I was on Medicaid and in my 20s, so every time I approached the subject with my nurse or my doctor, they would counsel me on why I probably should not have the procedure including what if I were to meet "Prince Charming" and he wanted a child? Or what if one of my children died, God forbid? Each time I argued that I previously thought I had met Prince Charming (twice) and they turned out to be "frogs" and now I had two children with two different fathers, and I can never replace either of my children with another child. After having this conversation multiple times, I also realized that they were obligated to counsel me each time. They were not refusing to do the procedure, so the next time they broached the subject, I told them to give me the documents. If they documented that they counseled me, they would be compliant with the state laws. I was well informed and signed a consent for 30 days before the procedure according to Medicaid rules. I had the procedure on my birthday as a present to myself in 1979. Since it was an ambulatory procedure, I went to celebrate that night with a little 'crampy' discomfort. I had a surgeon who was known for performing surgery with a very meticulous incision, and I only had a tiny scar on my belly button. I have not once regretted that decision.

Later, in 1979, L- asked if he could bring his teen daughter over because her mom threw her out for having a boyfriend. I agreed on the condition that it would only be until the end of her school year when she graduated. Boy, the Lord sure works in mysterious ways…

In March, the final straw with L- was when he came home one day and abruptly turned off the TV that my son was watching. We argued about it, and I wound up calling the police and having him escorted out of the house. The next day, I took his teen daughter and my children for a walk after changing the locks to the house. It was his birthday and as we walked away from the house, we saw him walking in our direction and the teen daughter said, "Oh no he's coming!" She had witnessed confrontations between her mother and him in the past and was afraid of the confrontation. I stayed calm and assured her there would not be any problem. As he walked towards me with a self-assured smirk on his face, I smiled back because I had changed the locks (with the help of neighbors) and put his belongings in trash bags in his car. He had taught me how to pick the lock on a car and by the time he reached the apartment and realized he could not enter it and then saw that his belongings were in the car, I was in another part of town with the kids. He was not there when we returned. Later that night he came back begging to be let in because it was his birthday, and it was a cold, rainy night. I stood my ground as the police had previously told me to. I have no rights if I let him back in and I didn't let him in.

He came to the house a few weeks later, and I said, "You know what she needs, like pampers and baby food. If you don't want to give me money for her needs…" while she was crawling around him in the foyer. His response was classic, "If I never supported the other six, why would I start now?" So, I just took my little tot and put her in the apartment. "From now on, I made her myself and you can just forget about her!" I slammed the door on him. Good riddance!

While his teen daughter was still with me, I enrolled her in the local YWCA gymnastics classes, which were barely affordable. That is when I enrolled in a new Domestic Violence support group for women. I couldn't relate as I watched woman after woman with various signs of physical abuse answering the facilitator, who said, "Think about what you want. Is it to leave this person?" One after another said, "I'm not sure...he is always so remorseful afterward" or

"He's so different when he doesn't drink." or

"I don't have a job and he pays all the bills."

I had it! I knew what I wanted! A plan for how to get him to leave me alone! The only thing that held me back was his constant threatening to harm my parents. I didn't want to put them in any danger, but I didn't want to be in this relationship as I pursued my nursing career.

At my home, I had befriended teen neighbors who were a little on the wild side and a little protective of me.

One day, I was upset with his daughter because she didn't want to go to her gymnastics class, and I had been scrimping my spare pennies so she could attend, but it turned out to be a blessing in disguise for me. When I answered the door that did not have a view, I assumed it was my friends visiting. All I know is that out of nowhere, I felt a blow to my face that was so powerful I lost my balance and then I heard L- over me, "You gonna call them now B-?" repeatedly, and with each question he was kicking my nose from the left with his construction boot until his daughter ran from the back of the house and startled him,"Papi, stop! Papi, what are you doing?" He was spooked as he ran out to a car that was still running. It was not his car and frankly, I think he came to kill me. She saved me! With all those kicks, I was lucky to not have any broken facial bones!! The whole left side of my face was black and blue. Of course, I did call "them" (the police) again, and they reminded me not to let him in the house again as if I needed reminding. He stayed away for several more weeks.

As June was nearing, I reminded his teen daughter that she would need to return to NY on graduation day. I knew her mom kept in communication with her dad, and she was always quite eager to gossip, so I devised a plan so that I could keep L- away from us. I convinced her and her mom that I feared L- so much that I was moving back to NY with my parents.

Stay tuned for the Escape in Part 2.

PART II: Mid Journey

Some people come into our life as
blessings and some come into your
life as lessons

Chapter Six

"I will either find a way or make one."

Hannibal

New Haven Years – 1978-1980

So, Dear reader, I last left you to wonder how I devised a plan to get out of my situation with L-. When I allowed L-'s teen daughter to stay with me in New Haven, I had stipulated that she would have to leave after her graduation in June. Well, I had the teen call her mother to pick her up after graduation. I had also asked Papi to come on the same day so that he could provide me with money to leave New Haven with my children. (These were the days before Cash App or Zelle) I had also spoken to my neighborhood teen friends to watch the apartment while I was gone. I planned to stay with my parents in New York and commute during the summer while I found another apartment in New Haven and applied for admission to Southern Connecticut State University (Southern) for the fall. So, on graduation day, "Baby Mama" showed up in New Haven with her new beau, but she conveniently did not have enough money for a Metro-North ticket for her daughter to return to New York. I had to ask Papi for even more money for the teen to go back home as well. We all took the same Metro-North train back to New York City, and I pretended to be terrified of L- and was therefore moving back to New York. I knew "Baby Mama" would convey the message to L- whenever she saw him, and she did.

Summer of 1980. While I was in the Bronx, I commuted to New Haven to look for an apartment and to apply to Southern Connecticut State University (Southern). On my visits, I not only found an apartment, but I went through the application process at Southern, and I'll tell you all about that later. My former neighbors watched the apartment until I was ready to move into my new apartment and in the first few weeks, L- made menacing calls to the apartment often and all they did was laugh in his face. My plan worked. After about a week, he stopped going to the apartment in New Haven and sporadically showed up at my parents' home in the Bronx. He would just skulk around across the avenue trying to get a glimpse of me or my daughter. He didn't have the nerve to confront either of my parents. I hadn't been around since I was in New Haven most of the time. I had found an apartment that was easy to commute to Southern.

God bless my parents! Papi was there to help me financially as well as emotionally. Growing up, Papi was never very handy around the home, but for the first time in I-don't-know-how many years, he came to help me put up curtains in my new apartment! I had never seen him with a hammer before. I guess he was so happy that L- was no longer in the picture.

From the beginning of my decision to go back to school in 1979, I researched the local nursing schools. In the 1970s, there were no easy ways to research other than to physically go to a library somewhere and look for studies and articles. I was doing my research while planning an escape from my domestic violence, as I previously mentioned.

After my thorough research, I applied to Southern Connecticut State University (Southern) in New Haven, CT. In terms of opportunities, there were two major institutions of higher learning that I was near, and they were Yale University and Southern Connecticut State University. Yale did not have an undergraduate nursing program, so that was out. Southern had a very robust baccalaureate program in nursing with an astounding passing rate in the NCLEX for nurses. From my new apartment in New Haven, I could commute to Southern and that's why I applied there.

The first person to interview me was a Latina in the Admissions office. I sensed hesitancy during her interview. I was not straight out of high school since I had been a young teen mom and by the time I applied to this institution, I had two children with the youngest just two years old. This interviewer did not even look at my previous transcript from LIU in New York and told me how the Nursing program was so rigid and generally accepted students directly out of high school. She then told me about two Puerto Rican students who were no longer in the program. "The previous students' history is irrelevant to me! I'm determined to become a nurse whether it is in your program or elsewhere... Now who can I speak to about getting admitted, since you cannot help me?!" She seemed a little taken aback, ruffled some papers, and referred me to her Director of Admissions who was a white male. He asked to see my transcript from LIU and, without blinking an eye, said, "I see you only need one more course in Physics to be in the Nursing program. So, do you want to begin in the summer, or do you want to start in September?" Just like that, I was in the Nursing program. The Director accepted all 95 credits from LIU, some of which were not related to Nursing such as 'drama' and 'piano' lessons. This was a bittersweet victory for me since I would have liked to have been supported by my own Puerto Rican colleague who, instead, tried to discourage me from entering the program. I wonder where I might have been if I had listened to her and not pursue my dreams. Over the years, this woman witnessed my success as I went through the nursing program and graduated since we were both part of the Organization of Latin American Students and she was related to my roommate. Although she was right about the rigidness of the program and the current dean, she knew nothing about my tenacity and determination. I also had two male mentors to encourage me along the way during this time. I do not have "warm and fuzzy" memories of my years at Southern, specifically with the Nursing department, but I do have warm feelings about my association with the organization of Latin American students and my sorority, Alpha Kappa Alpha Sorority, Incorporated. I became a soror in the Spring semester in 1984, the year before I graduated.

When I started at Southern, one of the first classes I took a driving course. The instructors were students who wanted to be instructors, and I had a great instructor for my group lessons. My friend/roommate bought a jalopy, and I used her car for my driver's license test. She would occasionally lend me her car to get back and forth. It didn't have such great tires, so I learned how to replace tires and every time I used her car, I wound up having to change the tires. My niece, who used to hang around school with me had been very proficient in auto mechanics in her high school. So, the two of us were often changing tires on this one car. I found it interesting that in New Haven, there was no 'damsel in distress' syndrome, like there is in New York. I would change a tire in the snow and other students would simply drive right by us without offering to help. None of us could afford AAA, so we had to figure it out. My friend benefitted because she was the 'girly' type and could not change the tires. It was good practice for when I got my car. Mostly, I relied on the buses to get me to and from school to pick up my children, except for that first semester when my daughter had to go to classes with me.

Reflecting on those years, I didn't think it was a big deal to just bring my toddler with me to class so that I could pursue my career. But it must have been quite a sight to see at a State University to have this one little person going from class to class with me. She was the only one. I know of one other classmate on public assistance at the time with children, but her 'baby daddy' helped her financially and with their care. She never had to bring her children to school. He sometimes drove her to school in his Cadillac. I remember feeling resentful because I was getting public assistance as it was intended, as a bridge to a destination, and not as a way of life.

Stay tuned for more of those crucial years on my journey to becoming a Registered Nurse with a Baccalaureate Degree (or two)

Chapter Seven

"Every saint has a past, and every sinner has a future..."

Oscar Wilde

The "Southern" Years -1980-1985

By the time I hit 25, I had already gone through the whole marriage and divorce thing. I was a single mom to two kids, hustling my way through nursing school. And let me tell you, my time at Southern was a real game-changer.

Between classes, I had these free periods, and I used them wisely, dear reader. I joined the Organization of Latin American Students (OLAS) and even held the position of treasurer. It was a wild adventure, meeting a variety of people from different backgrounds. It felt like my chance to relive those teenage years I missed out on because I was too busy getting hitched and having babies instead of exploring the dating scene and figuring out what I really wanted.

When I was 17, and I spilled the beans about my pregnancy on Mami, she threw out the idea of getting an abortion. But I stood my ground. I was determined to have that baby and get married. Mami just wanted me to experience the world, you know? To explore different relationships. Back then, I didn't get it. I thought I had found my Prince Charming already. But it took a few more years for me to realize how wise Mami was.

Let's get back to 1980, and it felt like I was living my teenage dreams all over again, with the added responsibility of being a mom. L- thought I was back in NY and stopped stalking me in New Haven. Most of my friends were younger than me, but I had the freedom to socialize during breaks between classes. I soaked up every ounce of that newfound independence. Hanging out with the OLAS crew, sipping wine, and treating myself to unique delights like coffee ice cream inside a freakin' cantaloupe.

Leaving behind that suffocating domestic situation, I was on the path to realizing my career dreams that I had always envisioned during my teenage years. I was popular among my friends, and I even dipped my toes back into the dating pool. Things were different, though. In my first year at Southern, my niece, seven years my junior, would come to visit me on campus. That's the same niece that always helped me change tires. Let me tell you, she caught the attention of some young guys. That led to a few casual relationships, you know, just for fun. But hey, I made sure it didn't mess with my studies. I saw those relationships as extra spice to my overall experience.

Looking back, I realize I couldn't have managed that same level of energy and balance between my social life and academic responsibilities now. Since I had already knocked out most of my liberal arts courses at LIU in New York, my first semester at Southern was all about electives. It gave me time to adjust to this newfound freedom. It was during that period that I met this older student in my psychology class who had me all captivated. We had this strong connection, made plans to hang out after class, but guess what? He stood me up. Turns out, the poor guy had gotten into an accident and was recovering at his ex's crib in Bridgeport, CT. Our relationship became sporadic after that, but I couldn't help still having feelings for him. I was smitten.

While he was out of reach, I sought physical connections with others, including this dude he called "Waldo." It was all about satisfying my needs while dealing with the emotional complexities of longing for the one I really wanted. I may have gone a little overboard. I'd call my crush's workplace non-stop, even after getting a talking to from the receptionist. But you know what? My persistence paid off. He didn't want me to stop calling. Eventually, though, our thing fizzled out, before I graduated in 1985 and I relocated back to New York. Except for this one unexpected encounter in 1986.

I was having a rough time with the person I was involved with one weekend, so I hopped in my car and drove aimlessly to Bridgeport, CT. Fate, or whatever you want to call it, led me to this multi-dwelling house where I bumped into my former crush. Can you believe it? We exchanged greetings, and he invited me inside. Turns out, he was supposedly 'helping' other young women like me by being their landlord. That meeting was exactly what I needed to break that spell he had over me. Even though he asked for a hug, it didn't spark any longing in me. I felt completely numb. That was the last time we ever saw each other, and the spell broke. So, let's get back to my years at Southern from 1980 to 1985.

During those years, my thing with "Waldo" remained purely physical. I knew what I wanted and made sure my needs were met. I'm grateful that I managed to navigate that time without any major consequences. AIDS was becoming a big thing back then, you know? But I made it through without being affected, thank goodness.

By the time I graduated in 1985, man, I had gone through multiple relationships and experiences. I'm thankful that I came out of it all unscathed. It was a transformative period that shaped me and prepared me for the challenges that lay ahead.

During my stint at Southern, I formed this tight bond with my bestie, "E," who had recently come out and embraced his true self. Before that, he had been living in the closet. He introduced me to the LGBTQ community, and we'd often crack jokes about our shared taste in men. My apartment became this happening spot for gay dudes, lesbian ladies, and even a transvestite, who had a serious Marilyn Monroe obsession. Can you imagine?

Through these connections, I got a real education about the LGBTQ community. We'd even hit up truck stops in West Haven where they'd meet their partners. At first, it was a bit tense, but I welcomed all these visitors with open arms, you know? We were all just people, and love is love.

Now, there was this one incident that stuck with me. My little toddler made this surprisingly mature comment in front of a couple of lesbian visitors. One of them then said that my kid might be gay. That comment got "E" all worked up, but me? I didn't see it as a big deal. I mean, I had this gut feeling that maybe my child would grow up identifying as a lesbian. She never showed much interest in girly stuff, always gravitated towards her brother's toys. So, I didn't react negatively to that suggestion. "E" still had some issues accepting himself at that point, I guess.

Anyway, my apartment turned into this cool hangout spot. All sorts of friends and acquaintances would swing by. But, man, there was this one big mistake I made that I still regret. I let this predator into our lives. Turned out he was a closeted gay dude who preyed on vulnerable women in our building, especially our neighbor with Down Syndrome. He took advantage of their money and emotions, and it was heartbreaking when I realized what was going on. I had to face my role in allowing that abuse to happen. It was tough, but I forgave myself and swore never to make the same mistake again.

And you know what? I had this unsettling experience with my upstairs neighbor, too. I had this feeling that she might've stolen a small envelope with a hundred bucks in cash. I couldn't prove it, though. But then, out of nowhere, an anonymous donor at my children's school stepped up and donated a hundred bucks. Can you believe it? I used that money to cover my children's tuition gap. It was a real lifesaver, for real.

Overall, my time at Southern really opened my eyes to different facets of the LGBTQ community. I had to face challenges with predators and sketchy neighbors, and I learned the hard way about self-forgiveness and growing from mistakes. It was a wild ride, but I wouldn't change it for anything.

I have to give a shout-out to St. Brendan's Catholic School in CT. They really came through for my kids and me, even when we were going through some tough times. St. Brendan's catered to the mid to upper class in the New Haven-Hamden area, and I was probably the only parent on public assistance. But man, those nuns, they took care of my kids until they couldn't handle my son's wild behavior anymore.

So, around 1984, I had moved away from my "LGBTQ" central and settled further away from our schools. One day, when I went to pick up my son from school, he was all hyped up and wanted me to come inside. I just wanted to catch my buses and head home, but he insisted. I gave in and went inside, only to find out that he had won "student of the month"! And guess what his prize was? A trip across the street to the supermarket with the nuns to buy groceries. But get this, he didn't choose candies and chips like most kids would. Nope, he went for the real deal- "chuletas" and produce, to make proper meals. I was blown away. It was unexpected, but in a good way.

The problem was, I had no way of lugging all the grocery bags home. I didn't know what to do. But those amazing nuns! They came through big time. One of them loaded up their station wagon with all the groceries and brought them to my home on the other side of town. Can you believe that? Despite my son's multiple suspensions from school, the nuns didn't want us to feel like charity cases. They were generous and kind, and I'll be forever grateful.

Oh, and let me tell you about another instance at St. Brendan's. My little girl was attending the school too, and one day when I picked her up, she was rocking a brand-new jacket with tags still on and everything! It was a hooded and insulated jacket in this cool grey and lavender combo. You know what's crazy? It was from an "anonymous" donor, too! I couldn't believe it. Just when you think life can't surprise you anymore, it throws a curveball like that.

Now, my spiritual journey, that's a whole other story. I started out in the Catholic Church because Mami thought my brother and I needed a solid foundation. But to be honest, neither she nor my dad were super religious. Mom had her beliefs, like her devotion to "La Virgen Milagrosa", the Virgin Mary and her love for Saint Jude, the patron saint of the impossible. Papi would prefer to speak with an "Espiritista", a spiritualist, if he had the chance, but Mami wasn't having it. We had to go to church every Sunday while in Catholic school, but as I grew older, I started questioning all the dogma. By the time I hit high school, I had moved away from strict Catholicism.

You know what? I had even considered becoming a nun at one point. Can you believe that? But then life happened, and I met this guy, and well, things changed. When my daughter came along, I wanted to get her baptized, but I had this misconception that because she was born out of wedlock, the church wouldn't do it. So, I went to the local priest to find out, and you know what he said? If I didn't marry her dad, my daughter could be baptized. Man, that didn't sit right with me. It felt so hypocritical, and it made me question the whole church even more.

During my time at Southern, I went through a bit of a rebellious phase relating to organized religion. But you know what? When I came back to New York after graduating in '85, something changed. I never lost faith in God's protection, but my concept of God evolved. I started exploring different theological principles and beliefs, and I realized that we cannot confine 'God' to one box. God is in all of us, and that's something I truly believe.

Anyway, looking back at those years, it feels like they lasted way longer than they did. But from around 1981 to 1985, I was juggling all these emotions. Trying to give my kids a spiritual foundation like my parents did for me while also working towards a better future for all of us. It wasn't easy being a single parent, but I always tried to give my children the best. I encouraged them to read, provided them with books and even made sure they knew about their roots, not just what the history books told them.

Honestly, a lot of those years are a blur to me now. But recently, my daughter and I had a heart-to-heart conversation, and she reminded me of things that I had completely forgotten. Like how I always got them subscriptions to "Highlights for Children" and made sure they had plenty of books to read. I didn't even remember those magazines! And as for my son, despite his behavioral issues, he's a smart kid with a talent for art. I discovered that when we moved back to New York in '85.

When I write about that era in my life, it's crazy to think about how much happened in such a short time. I always felt like my kids were cruising on autopilot, but talking to my daughter, I now see, I was also figuring out how to be there for them while striving for a better life. It wasn't always easy, but we made it through.

Next, I'll cover the challenges of academic life before the World Wide Web.

Chapter Eight

"The gem cannot be polished without friction, nor man without trials."

Chinese Proverb

University Life Before the Internet

O k, so enough about my extracurricular activities at Southern. We underestimate our present day "luxuries"! Ok, ok, so I didn't have to "walk barefoot 15 miles to school" like in the 19th century... But it is so much easier to research any topic in an instant or to take a course and become more marketable than ever. The "pandemic" has turned the world around even more since now we can go anywhere virtually. Zooms and other venues are common now and we can communicate with anyone around the world, 24/7. Who doesn't have a Smartphone nowadays? Even some homeless individuals have cell phones! Life moves forward at record speed today. If you have a question, any question, just 'Google' it. Now Google is a verb! You can be watching something on television and researching everything about the program at the same time. Everything is rushed... everything must be done now. There is no more waiting these days.

Travel back with me, if you will, to 1980 when I had a two-year-old and a seven-year-old in New Haven CT. I had just escaped a violent domestic situation, and I had orchestrated "my exodus" from New Haven to fool the perpetrator that I no longer lived in Connecticut. To communicate with my family, I would have to walk to the nearest grocery store to use the payphone. I moved across town in time to start at (Southern). As I mentioned before, I stayed with my parents in the Bronx, NY while I traveled back and forth to search for another apartment in New Haven, in a different part of town. This involved my having to make frequent visits to New Haven by myself until I found the apartment and finally moved in just before the semester began. I had been successful in my quest and my daughter's father thought I had relocated back to New York. I was now free to start a new life with my two children.

I moved to the part of town that was closest to a hospital in New Haven, St. Raphael's. I also learned how to navigate other areas of New Haven by public transportation, which involved using connecting buses at the "green" to get to the various sections. The green is the hub, within walking distance of Yale University.

Because my daughter was not quite two years and nine months old in September, they did not accept her in the childcare center at Southern, even though she was toilet trained. So, for my first semester at Southern, I needed to take her with me to my classes, after dropping off my son at his school that was on the way to Southern. I had to be very diligent with my scheduling of classes to accommodate for travel time in getting my son to and from his school and traveling with my little toddler. That first semester, I took my daughter to my classes with me and I was fortunate that she dealt with my classes the way she deals with life in general. When there's an issue 'just go to sleep'. This defense mechanism has worked well for her as well as for me. If I placed two chairs together, I could put her down for 'naps' in between classes, and she was fine. She was such a little trooper. She also grew an aversion to the health field since she attended so many of my nursing classes. Now, when she takes that nap, she wakes up "bright and bushy-tailed" and ready to conquer the world. It's basically a 'reset'. These were just some of the orchestrations of a typical day in the 1980s.

When doing research for any of my classes outside of the heavy textbooks I had purchased, I needed to go to the library physically and learn where to search for my topics. I became very familiar with the various libraries. I had to make sure I had plenty of coins if I wanted to make copies of my research to work on at home. Sometimes, I had to wait for articles that had to be requested and then come back to the library when available. Remember, there was no Google back then.

I remember being so grateful for having an IBM "Selectric" typewriter with carbon paper to have a copy of my term papers. The originals I submitted, of course appeared pristine, but the copies were horrendous because of the built in "White-out" on the "Selectric" that corrected them. Back then, we also did not have cell phones, let alone Smartphones. We always had to have coins to use the payphones until I could pay for a landline in my apartment. All of this makes for a very long day. I'm not even discussing times for preparing meals and helping my son with his homework. Fortunately, he was quite bright and did not require much help. His behavior was another story… he didn't deal well with authority and since I was only 17 years his senior, our interactions were more like sibling rivalry and Mami always took his side. He knew this and knew just how to manipulate us. If my research was not complete, I had to find my way to a library locally to further my research! More time that I did not really have.

By the spring, 1981, the Childcare Center at Southern accepted my daughter, which was open from 8:00 AM to 3:00 PM. Now I had different schedules to navigate since I had to make time for picking up my daughter from the childcare center on campus, then picking my son up off-campus and returning for any evening classes I may have. I picked evening classes where I could keep my children with me or right outside of the classroom. Some days could be very challenging.

I had time during the day to participate in extracurricular activities like the Organization of Latin American Students (OLAS). I met many of my friends through this organization and my mentor as well. Of note, that woman who tried to dissuade me from applying to Southern's Nursing program was also a member and close friends with my future roommate. It was a small organization, and they needed officers, and somehow, I became the treasurer. Yep, I also helped them design a logo for "OLAS". In Spanish 'olas' means 'waves', so I created a logo with the "S" forming waves over the word to flow over to the beginning of the "O". I wonder how long they used it.? Prior to my involvement, I think the organization was being run like a social club. At budget time, I had to create a budget to submit to the student organizations' board for approval. Policies and procedures were all drawn up, so I simply used them to draft the proposal. On the day of the presentation to the Board, I was so nervous because I wasn't comfortable with public speaking. Since the meeting was after lunchtime, I got together with some of the members, and had some wine instead of lunch to calm my nerves. It worked like a charm! Not only was I at ease during the presentation, but my budget was approved, and the approval was for a higher number than I had requested. I felt so accomplished, and this gave me the confidence to aim higher. I realized then that I had a very analytical mind and I suppose that spurred me on to my successes. I've had many in my nursing career. I found it very easy to just follow the directions and come up with a viable budget, but no one had thought to use the resources before. I am no smarter than anyone, but I am diligent and whatever I set my mind to do, I will do to the best of my abilities. Sometimes, I sell myself short and I don't really see what others see in me. My mentor saw back then that I had what it takes to succeed. I just thought I was doing what I was supposed to do.

In my third or fourth year, a fellow student approached me, and she invited me to pledge for Alpha Kappa Alpha, Incorporated sorority. Coming from the South Bronx with no immediate college students in my family, I had no clue what a Greek sorority or fraternity was. I was told that I could only pledge by invitation, and she was inviting me. In 1983, the former Southern Connecticut State College had just been certified as a university and they did not have AKA on the campus. Yale University did not have an undergraduate nursing program and did not have an AKA chapter. Xi Omicron chapter was a New Haven city undergraduate chapter, and the meetings were being held at Yale University, which was closer to my home. As I learned more about AKA as a sorority of college-educated women, I was more and more intrigued by the camaraderie of such an organization. "Sorority" means sisterhood in Greek after all. I remember hearing the "Big Sisters" talking about always having a "soror" anywhere in the world and if you ever needed anyone, anywhere you would be taken care of by your sorors. I believe in those years, they started recognizing Latinas as women of color, regardless of the color of their skin. One of my line sisters was also a Puerto Rican attending Yale university pre-law. It didn't matter that AKA was the first black woman's Greek sorority founded in Howard University in 1908. The more I read about the history, the more impressed I became with the vision of the sorority. Despite everything going on in my life and navigating my nursing, OLAS, and my children, I pledged. There was one accommodation that had to be made because twice a week, I had clinical rotations at Yale - New Haven Hospital and there was no way that I could carry around my little Ivy plant (we were required to always have during the pledging). My Big Sisters allowed the break only during those Tuesdays and Thursday clinical rotations. In February,1984, I became a soror of Xi Omicron chapter of Alpha Kappa Alpha Soroity, Inc. One of the requirements was that we must maintain a GPA over 3.0. So yes, I was still succeeding in my nursing pursuit. This was during the time when I had been reinstated in the Nursing department after the "issues" with my children.

Financially, I had to be a full-time student to qualify for work-study, loans, and any other scholarships like the Hispanic Heritage Foundation. Interestingly, my work-study position had been in the financial aid office. Since I had to repeat my last year, I basically exhausted all my financial aid. One of my clinical rotations was at Yale-New Haven Hospital, in my last year. The urology floor was short-staffed, and they liked me so much, they offered me a stipend if I would work on their unit a few hours as a student nurse. I thought this was a godsend, so I agreed.

Around the second or third year at Southern, we moved to another part of New Haven behind Yale-New Haven Hospital on the first floor of a house where the owner and his family lived as well. My friend and classmate agreed to move in for financial reasons. It wasn't until very recently, that I realized just how stupid some of my choices had been back then... There were three bedrooms on the first floor. I took one, my roommate had another, and my son had a bedroom. I wouldn't put my little girl in a bedroom with her male sibling, so I made some kind of makeshift bed in the foyer for her to sleep in! What was I thinking? My daughter and I were recently talking about our past and she reminded me of this situation. I am so remorseful! I always felt that I had not adequately provided for my children, and I particularly had a lot of guilt about not providing for my son or protecting him from my daughter's father and so I was always trying to "make it up" to him by giving in to a lot of his 'nonsense' and making sure he had the best room wherever we lived. My daughter was such an "old soul" and never complained and I suppose that is why I chose that ridiculous "solution" that I am not proud of at all.

I am also not proud of how angry I was in those days. I was not raised with corporal punishment, and I was not comfortable with hitting my children. Instead, I cursed and yelled a lot back then. My Special Ed student classmate once said, "I really don't like the way you curse at him!" I was very frustrated with all my obligations, and he wasn't making it any easier. I lashed out the only way I knew how and it's not an excuse, it's just facts about how it was back then. For all my mistakes, I don't regret many because there was learning to be had, but this period in my life I do regret, and I wish I could have handled the circumstances differently. I realize just how resilient my little daughter had been through it all.

During this time, I had pushed away from my Catholic upbringing and was not very enlightened or spiritual. I guess I was in "survival" mode until I could graduate and begin my career as a nurse. My son was continually getting into trouble at school, but his grades were stellar. One time, his grades faltered a bit, and he was behaving well in school. He said, "You can't have both, either good grades or good behavior." I had tried seeking counseling for my son in the past. Whenever we returned home from his sessions with the therapist, he became more unruly than ever. He would sometimes yell at the top of his voice so neighbors could hear, "Child abuser, child abuser!" I wasn't even near him, and I never hit him. I asked the therapist what to do, and he said, "Next time he does that, slap him and tell him I told you to." I don't remember if I did slap him, but I don't remember going back to that therapist again. When my little one was about six and he was about 11, I had clinical days on Tuesdays and Thursdays at the hospital across the street and I had to be there by 7:00 AM. I could not take them to school, which was across town, and I didn't have a car. We lived on the bus line that went to the 'green' to catch the bus that would take them to their school. I had to put them on the first bus as I was going to my clinical. During that time, my little one often had stomach problems and looking back now, it was obviously her nerves. Out of the blue, a woman came up to me one day, "I know it's none of my business, but do you know that your big one kicks your little one on the way to the bus?"

"What??????" I felt as if a bulldozer had just run over me. I saw "red", and I didn't know what I could do because I had to finish my clinicals, and they had to go to school, and I couldn't see any way out of this dilemma. I saw that one of the smaller buildings of the hospital across from our home was an outpatient mental health "clinic". I investigated and found that there were social workers who would counsel us. I asked for help. They evaluated us as a family and one of the social workers said she could not work with my son. She said she would be happy to work with me and my daughter and they would assign another social worker to him. I never knew why that social worker refused to work with him. They gave us positive reinforcement exercises and behavior modification tasks. Early on, they had my son "evaluated" by a male psychiatrist. After his consultation with my son, he interviewed me as well, but he seemed to have preconceived notions about me. He may have read the social worker's notes on the intake chart. I had voiced my anger with my son when I found out that he was abusing my little one, and I shared that with my social worker. I may have used the words, "I wanted to kill him!" That may have influenced this man's very condescending and judgmental demeanor towards me. "You do know that hitting your child is not appropriate?" He acted as if I was beating my son. I don't know what my son might have told him. This male psychiatrist then turned to my son, "You know it's not right to hit your little sister, right? And you are not going to do that anymore, right?" My son replied, "Right." as he nodded in agreement with a cherubic smile on his face. I believe my son successfully manipulated that therapist and I'm not sure what he wrote in his chart, but I was through with him. I asked the social workers to keep that man away from us. By the time I graduated and was ready to move back to New York, the social workers had concluded that my son had not learned boundaries and proper behavior. They felt he needed a structured environment in which to relearn behavior, such as in an Academy. Yeah, right, and who is going to pay for this? No thanks, some of our issues resolved once we returned to New York and my son was near his grandmother, Mami.

My roommate decided she could not live with us any longer. My son had kicked her away when she tried to calm him down during one of his tantrums. Mami tried to alleviate some of my child-rearing woes by coming over for a few days at a time, but that didn't really help. One day, my son refused to get ready for school and literally had me running around the perimeter of the house to get him ready.

He refused to get ready because he wanted to stay home with Abuela. Since I cursed so much, Mami believed I was chasing him to beat him, and I wound up arguing with her because I never did beat him or hurt him. Mami said, "Me voy. Yo solo puedo ver por sus ojos, y eso no te ayuda." She knew she was biased toward him, so she decided right then and there not to come back to New Haven to help me out. She said I would need to find a way to fend for myself. And that is what I did for the remaining year at Southern. Next is how I coped towards the end...

Chapter Nine

"Learning's a gift, even when pain
is your teacher..."

Michael Jordan

Maybe This Isn't for You

Now on the academic side, I was experiencing another set of obstacles to my dream of becoming a nurse…. "You only injured a finger… Try breaking your arm and being in a cast for a year…! You have no choice but to learn how to write with your left hand!" said the "Queen of Mean", my Psychology Professor. I had learned that I could assign a proxy to take an exam for me if I were incapacitated and since my right hand was now in a cast from an accident I had sustained, I went to her office to ask for the accommodation. I thought, "Surely this is just a formality." I just sat there momentarily with my mouth wide open and beads of sweat on my forehead. Two days before this class, I had been washing dishes in the evening and when I was rinsing a glass, the glass broke in half and severed my right index finger knuckle. I now have a permanent 'half-moon' scar on that joint as a reminder… Medical professionals make the worst patients, and I am no exception as a professional-in-training. There was a lot of blood, and I rinsed the finger with lots of cold water, kept it clean, and wrapped it up, but did not seek medical help.

The next day when I woke up, I felt a 'jolt' in that finger followed by excruciating pain! The bleeding had subsided with my makeshift bandaging. I knew I had to go see someone, so I went to the school nurse after getting my kids to their respective destinations. We never know how dependent we are on our senses until we lose the ability to wipe our butt effectively. The nurse sent me to the emergency room, but then I was told that because it had been over 12 hours, I would need to go to a plastic surgeon to repair the severed tendon in that first finger. There is an increased risk of infection after 12 hours post-injury. This is how I wound up with a cast on my right hand and I now could not manually write in my classes. I needed plastic surgery on my tendon! I wound up getting help with health insurance.

I don't remember how, but it came to my attention that proxies could be used when there was an incapacity to write in a class and that is how I decided I should speak to my instructor for this psychology class. I was in her class and there were no multiple-choice questions. Everything had to be written in essay form, including the exams. This was a particular challenge for me because I was very good with multiple-choice questions but was a little slower with essays, even with the use of my dominant, right hand. Back in the 1980s, we did not have Smartphones, dictation and the World Wide Web. I was 'lucky' enough to have an IBM Selectric typewriter for my papers. We take so much for granted. One cannot imagine just how difficult it is to have to go to a library and research papers and articles and make copies of whatever you need to go back home and try to compile everything. All this, while caring for two small children. Typing with one hand is not as bad, but when you must manually write in a class for your exam or for your notes, it's much harder to do it with your non-dominant hand.

I just couldn't understand the denial of this accommodation. This was for one of my psychology classes, my second major in nursing school. I cannot remember her name, but she was an alum of NYU and very proud of it. She mentioned it often enough. There she stood in her Teutonic and pompous manner, placing another stumbling block in my path to freedom. The smug look on her face seemed to say, "Let's see how you manage this one!" I was doing better in my psychology classes than in my nursing courses. I politely withdrew from her presence, fully determined to overcome this obstacle despite her lack of intervention. I doubt she knows the meaning of the word "empathy". It doesn't matter because I didn't need her empathy or approval. I was tenacious enough to teach myself how to use my left hand for writing and all my tasks.

I did not have to contend with this issue as well in my other classes. The other classes had quizzes and multiple-choice questions. I could just read and remember what I wrote the night before. I read for most of my classes, but hers was the only one that required all manual writing! My twenty-something-self did not think of questioning 'her majesty's' authority or appealing to her superiors. This was before the American with Disabilities Act. I'm sure there must have been some way for me to gain a proxy, but I just accepted her denial and moseyed on out of her office, determined to go home and teach myself how to write with my left hand. I didn't argue with her or try to prove my case. I just walked out of her office, momentarily feeling defeated. That was me then. Go home and have a good cry about it until the solution appears. I certainly had plenty of textbooks to practice taking notes with my left hand so that's what I did after I cried until there were no more tears left... (Let me try doing it now as I write in this notebook, ugh!) not that my normal handwriting is that great but at least presently I can dictate my words into a Word doc and make any corrections a lot quicker.

The present-day me would have gone to the office that provided the accommodation or I would have gone to the chair of the psychology department first. I might have gone to one of my mentors to see what other options I could have pursued. To this day, I don't know why this woman was so determined to see me falter. I had so much going on in my life that I was not aware if she was like this or if 'was it only with me?' The smirk on her face as I left her office made me feel it was only me, especially through my years at Southern. I avoided her at all costs, but the few encounters with her were less than pleasurable. Frankly, as I look back on this episode, I'm not sure how she accepted my work in my crude left-handed writing, but I obviously understood the subject and conveyed my knowledge adequately. It was so long ago that I can't really remember, but I finished her class with an 'A' or 'B'. I don't believe I had started my nursing courses yet. It wasn't until the second or third year that I had to approach "Queen of Mean" again on my application for the Health Sciences Certification in psychology and by then, I had a little more confidence in myself, except for that momentary lapse of insanity when her words stung me. Maybe all those months of writing with the right side of the brain strengthened me. The right side of the brain rules the left hand, which controls attention, memory, reasoning, and problem-solving. I must have thoroughly exercised those skills. I could reason with myself quickly and realized that there was a better way to resolve my challenges other than the suggested recommendations of that woman. I have forgiven her as the forgiveness frees me and doesn't condone her behavior. I am stronger for this experience.

Well, I'm not sure how, but I taught myself to write with my left hand immediately and took notes and my quizzes, and I still passed with flying colors. I also learned a new skill from this challenge, i.e., how to write with my non-dominant hand if I needed to... just not as quickly. I persevered, and I finished that semester successfully!

That was not my only encounter with "Queen of Mean" ... The psychology department had a Health Sciences certification concentration and since I needed additional credits to be a full-time student and qualify for scholarships and loans in my third year, I concentrated my second major into the Health Sciences Certification, which seemed appropriate for nursing and health care. To apply for the certification in psychology, I needed to speak to the dean, which just happened to be the 'Queen of Mean'. "Who do you think you are that you can do everything? No wonder you have so many problems with your children!" How did she know about my issues with my children? I was seeing therapists for them, but it was at the Yale Child Development Center, which had nothing to do with my State University. She continued her rant, "You should leave the nursing program and just get a psychology degree and get a minimum wage job to spend more time with your children... then later on when they're grown you can go back to nursing...!" For a nano-second only, I thought, "Oh my, I'm a terrible mother. What am I thinking?" In a split second, I decided she was a 'lunatic', and I questioned her credibility. I had invested my life in pursuing this nursing degree! I would finish nursing and forget about the Health Sciences track. After all, that certification was only 'icing on the cake' - it was not essential to me.

It really doesn't matter what that woman's motives might have been, I'm just thankful that I did not allow her to influence me to give up my dreams of becoming a nurse and being financially independent of public handouts!

It has not been an easy road to get into nursing school and stay there, with two small children and relying on public assistance, which was so shameful to me. Granted that my choices in life have brought me in this direction, but I saw my vocation as a nurse to serve and provide for my children in an honorable manner. Nursing was a calling for me, not just a means of making money.

I will always remember one of my first classes in nursing where the instructor told us to think about our patients as if they were our family members and how we would want them to be treated regardless of who that person was. Each person could be our mother, father, brother, sister, cousin, aunt, grandparent... You get the picture. Throughout my career, I never forgot this, and I feel it made me a better nurse.

I saw my years in school as an investment in myself. There was a destination that did not include public assistance, food stamps, and charity meals every six months. I did not want to just survive; I wanted my children and me to thrive! I dealt with guilt about my choices. I now had two children with different (absent) fathers, and it was up to me to provide for them. If I were to entertain giving up nursing and just getting a general Bachelor of Arts degree, which would qualify me for nothing, I could work at McDonald's and still must receive partial public assistance until my children grew up. With minimum wage, I would still need public assistance to help me out, and that could be indefinite. Once you are in the 'system', it's difficult to get out.

All my issues with my children wouldn't magically disappear, either. My son did not want to be living in Connecticut with me. He wanted to be with his grandmother in New York City and if I were just working a minimum-wage job, that situation would not be changing. It is likely he would be more disruptive and there would be childcare expenses, too. I could not bring my youngest to work with me like I did at school. I knew once I graduated with my BSN, I would be gainfully employed, and I could provide for my family without handouts.

I've witnessed generations of welfare moms and their daughters thinking this is a way of life and just continuing the legacy. I have also witnessed Papi working two and three jobs at a time to provide for us, so Mami would not have to apply for "welfare". When that professor made her suggestions, all I could think was, "I'll be damned if I have just wasted all these years trying to get out of the system and now stay in it!" I thought all of this at that moment when I just walked out of her office without applying for that Health Science certification. There were plenty of other classes I could take to remain a full-time student in the Nursing department and I decided that I would become a Registered Nurse with a Bachelor of Science degree. Nothing could give me greater pleasure than calling the social services office to tell them to close my case.

I simply took more psychology courses as long as she had nothing to do with them! I was so disappointed that an accomplished woman like her would not show compassion and empathy for another woman trying to succeed as well. I vowed that when I made it, I would do all I could to empower other women who were struggling. I had plenty of opportunities as a Registered Nurse and later as a Nurse Informaticist to mentor other nurses. It always gave me great pleasure to encourage other nurses to follow their dreams.

It wasn't all doom and gloom in those years. I had a few wonderful mentors, "angels" along the way, although none of them were women. Two were one of my early professors and the Director of Affirmative Action. These two men helped to propel me forward towards my goals throughout the years at Southern. There were specific times in those years when these two men selflessly helped me along the way. I knew, and so did they, that my focus was always nursing, and I was not to be veered from that track. No matter what obstacles arose, I knew that I could always turn to them for guidance. There were many instances throughout the years to dissuade me from finishing what I came here to accomplish. Whenever I sought guidance from my nursing instructors, I often met with, "Have you thought that perhaps this is not for you?" They all seemed so disingenuous. Throughout those years, all I could see was the finish line that would lead me to a career as a nurse so that I could be independent and take care of my children. Stay tuned for the final years and my reaching the other side of the Bridge.

PART III: Final

Just because you are struggling
doesn't mean you are failing.

Chapter Ten

"There is only one thing that makes a dream impossible to achieve: the fear of failure."

Paulo Coelho

I am a Palm Tree

L ooking back on those years, I'm not sure how I made it with all the challenges. When I started at Southern in September 1980, my youngest was barely two and a half years old and although she was potty trained, was still too young to enter the Child Development Center there. I wound up taking her to my classes with me and just putting two chairs together so she could take naps. Sometimes Mami would come from New York to try to help with the babysitting. That, however, was a double-edged sword since my older child was then about 10 years old and he only wanted to be in New York with his grandmother. He would act out because he did not want to stay in school while Abuela was visiting. Mami was a very wise woman and realized that coming to help me only made things worse with my son. As I previously mentioned, she decided not to come back to Connecticut to "help" and I would need to fend for myself. I was fortunate that at least, I had a roommate and some friends who would chip in to help in the last few years. That is, until it became intolerable for my roommate as well. I was at the mercy of any friends who would want to help with my child rearing for free. My only income was from public assistance, which barely covered rent and food. My parents subsidized the children's tuition. After the first year, my daughter was old enough to be accepted in the Child Development Center at Southern and that was helpful except for evening classes that I had because the center closed at 3:00 PM and I still had other classes. So, my daughter went to my classes with me in the evenings. She learned everything about healthcare by osmoses. It's no wonder that she wants nothing to do with health care. She was so saturated and turned off to anything medical. My son was a bit of a challenge in those years. He was creating havoc at the Catholic school that my parents helped subsidize. The school bus was on the route to my university. That's another story for another day. The nursing department was not always very accommodating either. I heard more than once, "Maybe this isn't the program for you..." If it weren't for the emotional and sometimes financial support I received from my parents and my mentors, it could have been a different story altogether. It would have been much easier to just quit but that word just isn't in my vocabulary!

By my third year at Southern, I could not pass a single quiz in the pediatrics rotation. Although my research and my papers were excellent, and I was excellent in my clinical rotation, I could not pass a single quiz. My instructor was certain there might have been an error with the quizzes. She knew I knew my content and I was excellent in clinical. But I just couldn't pass the cursed quizzes.! I think this was around the same time I had issues at home. In any case, I handled this the way I handle most of my challenges. I have a good cry. But while I'm crying, I am also brainstorming to build my bridge. I envision the 'wheels' of my mind intertwining until a 'lightbulb' pops up brightly with an answer!

Looking back on this time, I guess I was severely depressed, and I caught a cold that I couldn't shake. Because I couldn't pass those quizzes, I did not pass the semester and again I cried.... I was walking in the hallway at school when my mentor saw me, "How's my favorite nurse?", with his big bubble-gum smile. I started bawling right there. "I will NOT be a nurse...." We walked into his office so I could finish venting and collect myself. When I calmed down, I told him what had happened. "I am going to have to finish the Psychology course to get a degree and get a minimum wage job to survive until my children are older..." Just like the Queen of Mean had suggested. He said, "You know? The new dean of the school of nursing and you are going to meet. And you will explain the situation to her so she can reinstate you. She will understand." He insisted, despite my misgivings, and I did speak with her.... She was such a stark contrast to the previous authoritarian dean. She listened to me empathetically and when I was finished with my sniffling dialogue, she simply stated, "Write what you just told me in a succinct manner, and we will present it to the school board. And you can start back in the nursing program next semester." The sniffles instantly stopped and all I could say was. "That's it?" Just like that, I was back on track… well, a year later, because the pediatrics course was only offered once a year. My mentor knew the dean and he knew she would listen and make the right decision. She had also been a single mom. I am indebted to him for the rest of my life! This time, he helped me continue on the bridge. I am indebted to my dean as well for that second chance. The previous dean would not even have entertained an explanation. There were no second chances with her. I was so engrossed in trying to complete my studies that I had not even noticed there was a new dean until my mentor insisted that I speak with her. My cold disappeared just as quickly as it had appeared. It has been said. "The greater the difficulty, the more the glory in surmounting it." ~Epicurus. And my saga at trying to become a nurse against all odds continued...

After my reinstatement, I did not have any more issues with any quizzes. I passed them all. The Universe conspired on my behalf to help me to continue my journey. The fact that my mentor knew about the new dean of nursing and the fact that I faltered after she was there instead of when the other authoritarian dean was there were not coincidences. Thank God, I was not the third Puerto Rican to be ousted out of the nursing program. Looking back on 1985, I think I was the only person of color in the nursing program to graduate. I didn't look at the world in terms of color (race). I was not trying to prove anything to anyone. I just knew that I had to fulfill my destiny. Before I graduated, I was invited to be on a panel of speakers at an event by OLAS and I got to share that I was about to graduate with two job offers in nursing at two prestigious hospitals in NYC. One of the Puerto Ricans that had been removed was at the event and she was so supportive and happy for me.

Prior to that semester, I purchased an old, red Chevy Malibu for $500 cash and I drove it home but as soon as I parked it, it would not restart. New Haven is unlike New York, where every other street or neighborhood has an auto mechanic. I could not afford to have anyone come to check my car or to tow it to a garage, and my landlord let me keep it on the grounds. At school, my next clinical rotation was a homecare rotation, and the homes were not located in accessible neighborhoods. They had an area in Branford, CT to the north with several homes that could be visited for the rotation, but I had no way to get there. I had to ask for some kind of accommodation - yet another time when I was told that maybe this field was not for me. After much discussion, there was another classmate who was asked to pick me up and we would be assigned cases in the same vicinity. I'm grateful to that classmate for taking on the additional responsibilities of getting me to Branford, CT, and back. I could sense her reluctance, understandably. We survived that semester, and we passed it. I am very grateful for all these experiences, which made me even more determined to reach my goal of becoming a nurse. I'm sure it was a challenge for her to pick me up in New Haven and take me to Branford and do her visit(s) and wait for me to finish mine and then take me back to

New Haven on those days (twice a week). My jalopy sat in my landlord's yard for about a year before a friend from New York visited and realized it was an alternator problem that kept the car from starting. My brother didn't visit very often, but he did one day. He was a very handy person, and he purchased an alternator and installed it in my car to make it work. That was just before I graduated in 1985. That semester was the only one where I needed transportation since I lived behind Yale-New Haven Hospital, and I could walk to all my other clinical rotations. The city bus literally stopped in front of my entrance door, and it connected to the 'green' where the other buses were that went to Southern and my children's school. Physically, I was able to get to all my classes and rotations. It was all the other distractions that made those years even more challenging.

Sometimes my classes clashed with my children's school schedule and several times I needed to bring both to wait outside my classroom. My son was older and would not sit quietly outside. He was extremely noisy and disruptive. My younger one was no longer taking naps while I was in class. Not only could I not concentrate, but they were disrupting my classmates, which gave me a lot of angst. I simply had no other choice.

I was reminded of those awful times later, when I was working in New York and that classmate who drove me to Branford started working at the same hospital I was at. She asked me, "How is your horrible son?" I thought, Yikes! That really stung!

I guess I must be thankful that Southern allowed me to bring my children to school back then. I didn't have a partner to care for them and I didn't have enough money to pay for a sitter. Mami had bowed out gracefully and my roommate had moved out before her graduation because she couldn't tolerate my son's behavior anymore, so I really had to fend for myself that final year.

With all the storms in life, I really am a palm tree. I'll bend but I won't break!!

It was far from smooth sailing to graduation, but I persevered because failure simply was not an option.

Chapter Eleven

"It's wild that when you decide you're worth more, the Universe starts opening doors to make it a reality."

Cory Allen

Final Semesters-Weathering the Storms

S o now we are in my final semesters and one of my clinical rotations at Southern was on the Urology floor at Yale New Haven Hospital and they were short-staffed. They didn't have enough RNs (there was a nursing shortage in the US in the 1980s) and I was paired up with a seasoned LPN. I learned a lot about preparing patients preoperatively and following up with them postoperatively. The bulk of the patients were men with BPH which is Benign Prostatic Hypertrophy or an enlarged prostate. There were also other men with Erectile Dysfunction, usually because of diabetes who were admitted for penile implants. The universe seems to have a sense of humor since I wound up on this floor during my peak sexual years while in my 20s. I had one patient who required his blood pressure taken before going in for his BPH surgery and it was high. I took it a second time thinking maybe I had heard it incorrectly, but it was still very high, and he didn't have a history of high blood pressure. I asked if the LPN could check it to verify it really was high, but when she checked, it was normal. He was clearly reacting to me, so I asked to be reassigned. He went for his surgery as scheduled. I did not see this patient again until the day he was ready for discharge when he yelled out to his roommate, "This is the nurse that raised my blood pressure!" as he laughed. I was so embarrassed, and my LPN supervisor just found it humorous. The patient's wife had asked me how I could work there looking at penises all day. Frankly, I was not uncomfortable, and it was a learning experience.

Another elderly wife once asked me what I planned to specialize in when I graduated and I responded "Pediatrics" which is what I thought I wanted until the woman smiled hesitantly and said, "Have you ever thought of working with the elderly? You are so good with them." In that very instant, I knew that I would work with older adults since I have such an affinity for them. Her kind eyes and smile reassured me that this was the right decision. I felt very comfortable on this floor and even dealt with comforting a family member when one of my patients had to go on life support. I had to translate for the spouse since she only spoke Spanish. It was so emotional for me, but in retrospect, this transaction helped me when Papi transitioned many years later, and I needed to translate for him to accept that he was dying.

The supervisor on this floor was so impressed and she offered me a part-time position with a stipend. I had exhausted all my financial aid since I had an extra year to complete, and I thought this was a blessing, so I accepted. It was very convenient for me to take this position since I lived right behind the hospital. She had asked me if I would have any problems with public assistance and I didn't think I would. I wasn't concerned since I didn't have my face-to-face certification scheduled until the spring. I think I worked for a few weeks, and I was so grateful to have a little extra money to pay tuition and purchase my books.

I had felt so accomplished and hopeful about my work on the urology floor. I was learning so much more than the theory of nursing. I was experiencing a true calling. I thought I was so close to realizing my dream of making my own salary and providing for my children. My sense of compassion and caring were on full blast these weeks despite any issues with my current finances and childcare. But then, in an instant, I received correspondence from social services asking if I was "still working" at Yale New Haven Hospital? I felt like I was punched in the gut! I immediately contacted my supervisor at the hospital and told her I could not continue, and she was very upset with me, "I asked you if there would be a problem when you took the position!" I guess I had been in denial and thought it was a great opportunity to hone my skills and help pay for my education without thinking of the consequences. I responded to the state that I was no longer working at Yale New Haven Hospital and there was no issue with the funding, but now I had to think about what I would do to pay for my final semester fees. As I was getting closer to graduation, I researched where I would work when I returned to New York. I belonged to the nurse's student organization, and they provided tips on interviewing skills. I was also continuing my practice of visualization. I envisioned myself asking the interviewer questions like the article had provided and not discussing salary at the interview. On the scheduled date, I arrived at Columbia Presbyterian (where I was born) equipped with a set of questions about the position, and the interviewer was very impressed with my questions. She stated no one had ever asked questions in interviews before. She felt I would be suited to one of the floors (once I graduated), and she said if I didn't like it there, I could choose another floor. So, I had a job offer before I even graduated. Now if I could only pay to stay in school until I graduated!

Before that semester was over, the nursing students were invited to NYU Medical Center for a group interview. Of course, I participated. In the 1980s, NYU Medical Center had a new 'electronic' Physician Order Entry system which allowed nurses to complete orders without having to decipher doctor's orders manually. An MD could write an order on one floor of the hospital, and it would print out on any floor where the patient was. I found this fascinating. I already had a nursing position at Columbia Presbyterian when I graduated, but this technology and the environment lured me. I applied during the group interview, and they accepted me. I had not graduated yet, and I had two positions secured. I had to learn to draft my first letter to decline the original offer at Columbia Presbyterian. I would begin my first job as a graduate nurse at NYU Medical Center in June 1985! I would take the

NCLEX to become an official Registered Nurse later in October.

It seemed my dreams were aligning while my family was still being seen by the Development Center at Yale New Haven Hospital, to help with my son's erratic behavior, which appeared to have subsided somewhat. After his expulsion from Catholic school, he flourished in the public school system. He had not done well with the structure of the parochial school system. In public school, he was free to do as well or as badly as he wanted. He blossomed without the added pressure. As a matter of fact, at the very first parent-teacher meeting in public school, the review of his behavior and his grades were stellar. I could not believe what the teachers were telling me about my son, and I asked them to verify his Social Security number to make sure that we were speaking about the same child.

All was looking bright for me, but when I had to give up my stipend at Yale New Haven Hospital, I had a new stumbling block! As I walked through one of the hallways at Southern, one of my previous instructors greeted me and I began to sob like I always do when I can't see the solution readily. He whisked me away to his office and asked me, "What's the matter? Are the children OK?" I was speechless while I was sobbing. I managed to compose myself enough to explain that I had exhausted all my financial aid, and I would not finish my degree. Since I had to repeat that pediatrics rotation, I was one year behind, and I had used up all my financial aid, including loans. He said I should go back to the financial aid office, and I was reluctant since I had worked in that office for my work-study program, and I knew that there was nothing more they could do. He refused to accept this and called the Director of Financial Aid himself and demanded that I be seen and that they find funds for me, "You can't tell me that this young single mom, who has sacrificed the last few years cannot be helped this final semester!" He secured an appointment for me for the next day. When I went for my appointment, they told me that there was indeed a scholarship from the "Women of the War of 1812". I had never heard of them and didn't know why I would be a candidate for their scholarship. My final semester would now be paid for so that I could graduate. Praise God! Another miracle and now this storm was averted. It's amazing what happens when you remain focused on your goal and act on it. I was truly blessed to run into my former instructor on that day. I am forever grateful for his intervention. I have been blessed with these "angels" that supernaturally appeared for me. If it were not for my mentor who had convinced me to speak to the new Dean of Nursing when I was at risk of being taken out of the program, I would not even be at this stage of the game.

I now had help with my tuition, but how would I purchase my needed texts? Again, angels appeared mystically! My mentor came along again and one of my other friends paid for my final semester of books. I kept in touch with my mentor to date, but I lost touch with my friend after I moved back to New York. I once tried to find him via social media but did not find him. I recently 'googled' him and was directed to his obituary! He just passed away in February of 2021 and I never got a chance to show him my appreciation for his help in 1985. He was only 69. May he rest in peace. He had been a respiratory therapist at Saint Rafael's Hospital, and we met when I lived across the street from the hospital just before I started my pursuit of a nursing degree. He was such a charming friend, and he made the best sweet potato pie on earth! He said his secret was to add just a dash of Amaretto, but I think it was his own special love that he added. I have never been able to replicate that deliciousness. I also learned to eat coffee ice cream with him when he once served it up in a cantaloupe, of all fruits. It's still my favorite flavor although now it's plant-based ice cream. I was stunned by this news, as if we had just hung out. He had worked at Saint Raphael's 40 years before he retired, and the lovely messages from his coworkers were a testament to what a beautiful soul he was. I wish I'd thought of looking him up sooner.

I will forever be grateful to those special angels in my life who helped me on my journey to becoming a nurse.

Chapter Twelve

"Let gratitude be the pillow upon which you kneel to say your nightly prayer. And let faith be the bridge you build to overcome evil and welcome good."

Maya Angelou

The Other Side of this Bridge

Yay! I did it! I graduated on May 25, 1985, with my Bachelor of Science in Nursing (BSN) degree and the Army Nurse Corp awarded me the first Perseverance Award at Southern. I couldn't wait to leave New Haven, CT fast enough. My first day as a Graduate Nurse in NYU Medical Center in New York City was June 6, 1985. I contacted my social service worker to let her know I would no longer need public assistance and to stop sending food stamps as of June 1st since I would no longer live in New Haven. That was the most satisfying notification I have ever made. I gathered my friends and boyfriends and anyone that I could to help me hire a U-Haul truck from New Haven CT to Bronx NY. So, on June 1st, 1985, I collected my children and cat and my friends, and we used a U-Haul truck and my red Chevy to get to Bronx NY. I didn't even have time to properly take my children out of school. We just showed up in the Bronx and had them start school in NY. We put a few things in storage and my children would stay in the Bronx with my parents and I moved to Brooklyn with my cat to my friend's place. He had stayed with me in New Haven his last year at Southern and had agreed to give me a place to stay until I found my own apartment in New York. I was so excited to buy a uniform for my new job as an RN. My first job as a staff nurse was on an orthopedic floor that serviced the NY Yankees and many senior patients with fractured hips. I now cared for the older adult population I loved so much. An excellent way to start my career. Although this is the end of my story at age 30, it was the beginning of a new life for my children and me. My incorrigible son once said that I would be nothing but a student forever. I think he was so surprised when we set out to Bronx, NY, where he always wanted to be, and I really had a job! Once in NY, he was in his favorite place. He became less unruly and flourished in junior high school and High School. I remained focused through all my trials and tribulations, and it paid off. In October, I passed my NY NCLEX and received my Registered Nurse license!! My son blossomed in Junior HS and graduated from Columbus HS in the Bronx and my daughter went to the local Catholic school and eventually graduated from the prestigious Cardinal Spellman High School! I had a successful career in nursing and at age 50 I got a master's degree in nursing informatics from Columbia University (with some new trials and tribulations -but that's another memoir).

My favorite lyric by Donnie McClurkin in "We Fall Down" is:

"We fall down. But we get up. For a saint is just a sinner who fell down, And got up."

D ear Reader, thank you so much for taking this journey with me. I authored this book for you. This memoir took so long to write because I needed to re-live traumatic events to convey my message that there was always a light at the end of the road. I know my traumas may not be as severe as some of yours, but I want you to know that you can surmount any of them. You may need extra support from friends and/or professionals, but you must allow them in. Don't try doing it alone. It is so amazing how the Universe conspires on your behalf as soon as you make your desires known with gratefulness. I took writing 'breaks' (up to weeks at a time) periodically to reset my emotions, but I wanted to share my experiences with those of you who may not see a way out of your situation. There is always a solution to every "situation". (I do not believe in "problems" except in mathematics.)

If you have ever doubted that you can realize your dreams, whatever they may be, I am here to tell you that the power is within you. Success and winning are all subjective. My definition of success, when I was a young single mom, was to become a nurse, but it could have been anything, and I still would have been just as persistent. I hope I have been able to light a spark of hope in you. Don't let anyone define you or deter you from your dreams. I don't know where I would have been if I had listened to that admissions officer at Southern or the "Queen of Mean" in the psychology dept at Southern. I also don't know where I would have been without all the angels the Universe sent me and still sends me.

If a teen dropout and single mother like me can turn into a professional RN with a bachelor's degree despite some unwise choices in life, anyone can. There is always a way. Your present situation is not the destination.

Keep going!

With Love and Light,

Iris Virgínia Fernández

CONCLUSION

"New beginnings are often disguised as painful endings."

Lao Tzu

EPILOGUE

"My dark days made me strong or maybe, I was already strong, and they made me prove it"

Emery Lord

Dear reader, sometimes ten years can seem like an eternity while you are in it once you reflect on the lessons learned. It is amazing how much growth can be jam-packed into that one decade. I hope a few of these snippets that I've shared with you can serve as learning points for you as well.

At the very beginning of this journey, I realized that Mami only had my best interests under her guidance. When she counseled me, her wisdom was trying to save me from undue suffering. Of course, I also inherited her tenacity and perseverance, so I had to learn when to let go and just listen and when to pursue my dreams relentlessly.

Throughout that decade, I also honed my intuition. I learned to pick up on red flags when dealing with the men and friends in my life. I still needed some more lessons in the following decade, but that's another story. I think that sobbing incident when I began my relationship with L- was my intuition telling me I was approaching a challenging time in my life.

My greatest lesson was that I don't need to solve every issue alone. The Universe provided help along the way across this bridge, from my family (my parents and sister) and the nuns at St. Brendan's school to the mentors at Southern and many others who helped along the way. My sister and nieces helped me to navigate a new city with new rules so that I could learn to support my children. My parents helped me with their small financial contributions whenever they could. The 'anonymous' donors at my children's school all assisted me in continuing my journey. My mentor urging me to speak with the dean of the nursing school was a pivotal time in my pursuit of my degree. My other mentor insisted that financial aid be provided in my last semester and that allowed me to persevere.

They all strengthened me to pursue my career while raising my children to adulthood during my "Terrible Twenties". I think it was a blessing that I finally had my degree the year I turned 30! It's like I had graduated into adulthood at the same time.

I am finally free from the "welfare" system and have been able to serve others, as a nurse and as a mentor, throughout the years since my graduation.

Dear Reader, remain focused on your dreams and aspirations! Let nothing and no one deter you and you, too, will prosper!

Thank you for sharing my joys and sorrows, laughter, and tears.

In light and love,

Iris Virgínia Fernández

About the Author

Iris V. Fernández stands as a testament to perseverance and dedication. Navigating the challenges of the 1980s as a single mother, she expertly balanced her roles, providing for her children while pursuing an education in nursing. Iris's remarkable journey spans from her tenure as a staff nurse in a New York City hospital to pivotal roles in third-party insurance, all the while prioritizing the healthcare needs of the Latino community.

Her contributions as a diabetes educator, paired with her innovation as a research nurse in a telemedicine initiative for the elderly, highlight her unyielding commitment to positive change. An esteemed graduate of Columbia University, Iris boasts a master's in nursing informatics. For 15 years, she served as a clinical analyst, mentoring fellow nurses in nursing informatics at premier Magnet™ hospitals.

Upon her retirement in 2020, Iris embraced her passion for writing. As a co-author and founding member of Latinas 100™ Vol II and III, and a contributing author to Hispanic Stars Rising Vol III and IV, her writings amplify the voices of women, advocating for empowerment and representation. Additionally, Iris finds joy in the culinary arts, often 'veganizing' her favorite traditional dishes.

A vehement advocate against domestic violence, Iris lends her support to organizations like Break the Silence. Her compassion extends to animal welfare, fervently backing sanctuaries and rescues such as The

Sato Project, Skydog Sanctuary, Sheldrick Wildlife Trust, NY Bully Crew, and The Pug Queen.

For a deeper dive into her journey and endeavors, visit https://www.irislablanca.com.

PUBLISHED WORKS-ANTHOLOGIES:

Latinas 100™ LEAVING A LEGACY & INSPIRING THE NEXT GENERATION: USA English Volume 2, Adriana Rosales Haro

Latinas 100TM: Leaving a Legacy Inspiring the Next Generation, vol 3, Adriana Rosales

Hispanic Stars Rising Volume III: The New Face of Power, Claudia Romo Edelman

Hispanic Stars Rising Volume IV: The New Face of Power, Claudia Romo Edelman

Reflections and Notes

Reflections and Notes

Reflections and Notes

Reflections and Notes

Reflections and Notes

www.ingramcontent.com/pod-product-compliance
Lightning Source LLC
Chambersburg PA
CBHW071359120626
46546CB00002B/750

* 9 7 8 1 9 5 9 4 7 1 3 5 6 *

"Ever wonder why Paul said that 'the greatest of these is love?' Ed Gross personally and pastorally reveals the simplicity and complexity of love. Read his words, listen to his heart, and you will find yourself drawn to a deeper love for Jesus Christ and for other people. This is a book to move your heart, so be prepared to change and to love it."

Dr. William Krewson, Faculty, School of Divinity, Cairn University

"This is a helpful book, wise and spiritually alive, intended for use in personal devotions or small group studies, and reminding us of the love of God as the great theme that stands at the very core of Christian faith and life."

Dr. Gary D. Badcock, Faculty of Theology, Huron University

"This in depth, biblical study of the love of God will not only broaden your knowledge of this wonderful subject but will challenge you to look honestly at your own practice of true biblical love. Read it carefully, especially with a desire to apply its teaching to your own life, including your relationship with God and with others."

Dr. George Murray - Former Chancellor and present Stephen Olford Professor at Columbia International University

"Ed Gross is a thoughtful pastor and a good scholar. But this little book doesn't come from Ed's head, it comes from his heart; and to read it properly you need to open your heart and let it be bathed in the love of God. Ed himself will tell you that there is nothing new in what he writes-but it is a message we need to hear over and over, and it was a joy and encouragement to let Ed's passion touch my soul deeply."

Rev. Stephen Smallman – Late Author and Director, Birthline Ministries

"Agape love demands that we step outside of our comfort zones and be willing to sacrifice for those who often spit at us in return. It is the love modeled by Christ on the cross, when he said, 'Forgive them, Father ' It is impossible for us to give this kind of love unless we have first experienced such a love from God. Sadly, we as the church often do a poor job in modeling what we have received in abundance. Pastor Gross, though, reminds us that once we have experienced this kind of love from Christ, it ought to be impossible for us not to share such love with others."

Dr. Win Groseclose Westminster Presbyterian Church Rocky Bayou Christian School

"The first epistle of John states - herein is love, not that we love God, but that he first loved us.... This reality allows for us to approach Christ's summary of the Decalogue - love God and love our neighbor, with intentionality. Ed Gross helps us understand these truths in very practical ways using a simple, non-technical language in doing so. I would recommend this book to all generations."

Pastor Zachary Ritvalsky – Vice President of Institutional Alignment of Lancaster Bible College

"As a local church pastor, it is my supreme task to assure parishioners are on a spiritual growth track that leads to ... spiritual maturity in Christ. Such I believe is accomplished through multiple ministry mediums, even guest pastors ... invited to minister in my local church context .... At a Sunday morning worship service ... Pastor Ed Gross spoke ... on the topic of 'Let Love Win Through You.' The message's content and delivery, most certainly propelled by God's Spirit, created a spiritually attentive and sobering atmosphere that obviously resonated with the hearts of congregants and even inspired a post-message response of many who acknowledged an immediate need for transformation in their love relating to God, oneself or others. The challenge of the message resoundingly reminds Christians in any church or ministry context of the chief priority of loving God and others 'purely' and therefore 'triumphantly' in the whole of their living and service for Christ. Apart from such our pursuit and practice of Christian love is lost at the heart level."

"'Let Love Win through You' is destined to be one of God's tools of the twenty-first century which universally sharpens Christians' perspective and practice ... of Agape, providing elements of healing and health to hearts and lives in need of God's renewing love."

Pastor Ronald Parks Philadelphia Bible Fellowship Community

As Ron has just testified, Ed loves to preach and teach on the theme of Christ's love. He is available to speak for you in Sunday sermons, Saturday workshops or weekend conferences/retreats.

Contact him through his website - www.disciplesgo.com.